THE BATTLE AGAINST YOURSELF

Take Control, or Be Your Own Worst Enemy

Greg J. Vogt

The Battle Against Yourself: Take Control, or Be Your Own Worst Enemy

Published by Greg J. Vogt

ISBN: 978-0-692-83315-5 (paperback)
ISBN: 978-0-692-83317-9 (ebook)
LCCN: 2016963461

Disclaimers

Facts, Description, and Organizational Disclaimer:

I have tried to portray events, locales, and conversations from my memories of them. In order to maintain their anonymity and privacy, I have changed the names of individuals, places, institutions, and organizations. I have changed identifying characteristics, and details such as physical traits and properties, occupations and places of residence. The reader should not consider this book anything other than a work of literature.

Medical Disclaimer:

This book is not intended as a substitute for the medical advice of physicians. The reader should regularly consult a physician in matters relating to his/her health and particularly with respect to any symptoms that may require diagnosis or medical attention.

Nonfiction Disclaimer:

This is a work of creative nonfiction. The events are portrayed to the best of my memory. While the stories in this book are true, names and identifying details have been changed to protect the privacy of the people involved.

To my brother, mom, dad, and dear friend Evan.

Special thanks to my mentor for being the first person I talked to about writing this book.

Contents

Introduction

If you have never done something in your life that somehow affected both other people and yourself, then go ahead and close this book. Never open it again. Throw it in the trash if you please. But if you have done something that somehow affected both yourself and other people, then I encourage you to keep reading. No matter how small or large that thing was. This is the story of how I put myself in a position of having to overcome major adversity. This journey will take you on a ride from low points to high points. I was forced into trying to figure out how to salvage my own mistakes and work through them on a personal level to improve my life to where I envisioned it to be.

1

A Ball and a Hoop

Our house overlooks Central Elementary School in the bright and sunny city of Simi Valley, California. There are just four of us living in the household, three of them being some of the most important people in my life. My mother, Kari, is the sweetest lady I have ever known. The compassion, love, and charm she brings every day of her life is beautiful. My father, Rick, is my inspiration and the hardest worker I have ever seen. He puts his family over everything and gives us great guidance. My nineteen-year-old brother, Josh, is one of my favorite people. He is funny, ambitious, and charismatic. He is my best friend. Then there is me, who most people would describe as a normal college kid.

I was born in 1993, but my journey really began in 2001, when I was in the first grade at Central Elementary School. I was a young boy who enjoyed learning in school while having fun making new friends. I used to wake up every morning excited for school, not because I was going to be sitting in a classroom, but because I knew it was a guarantee that I would be playing basketball with my friends at recess. My friends loved basketball, and I took a strong interest in the game at an early age. I became a Los Angeles Lakers fan by age seven and would never miss watching a game. At school, my friends and I would play pickup games every single day during lunch and recess.

The two best players would always be team captains and choose whom they wanted on their teams. I was a decent player but not that good, so I would always be one of the last picks, if not the last. I would get frustrated because I thought I was worthy of more than that. When I wasn't picked dead last, I would get really excited. But no matter what, once those teams were picked and we started playing, I always gave it my all. I tried to do anything I could to help my team win every game, even though I wasn't really much of an asset. I usually had fun every time I was out there on that court, win or lose.

As we grew older together and reached the fourth grade, our basketball games elevated to a higher level of competition. Our games would often result in shouting matches because of some conflict. The kids were getting more skilled but also building more desire to win. Sometimes when I would play with really good players, I would get a little nervous and make a stupid play every now and then, a reoccurring play. I would drop the ball when it was passed to me. I don't know why this happened other than the fact that I felt pressure from the good players. Whenever I would drop the ball, the kids came up with a new nickname. They would call me Greasy Greg. I hated this with a passion because it made me feel inferior to them, but I never told them to stop. Every single time I dropped the ball, I would hear a sarcastic scream from every person on the court: "Way to go, Greasy Greg!" It came to the point that I grew excited for the school bell to ring because I no longer enjoyed playing basketball with my friends and would rather just be in a classroom.

Elementary school ended, and I was off to the next phase—middle school. I was excited for a change. I was going to school with the same kids, but also with new kids from another elementary school. I thought that with a new school, new kids, and chances to meet new girls, this could be a good change. I enjoyed middle school for the most part and liked meeting cute new girls. I worked hard in school and tended to succeed academically. I made new friends while keeping most of my old ones. I still played basketball at every break during school, and yes, I was still called Greasy Greg. I just went along with it and pretended to take it in stride, despite hating it. I had to deal with my best friends calling me that name, new kids that I would meet, girls using it as if it were my normal name, and even my teachers using it on a regular basis. Everyone knew me as Greasy Greg.

During middle school, I decided that I wanted to improve my basketball skills in preparation for high school. I joined a travel club basketball team called the Defenders. I ended up playing on the Defenders between the sixth and tenth grade. We would go all over California to play competitive teams. We played in big tournaments as well. I had two great coaches, Elijah and Tad, who taught me how to perfect the game of basketball and master the fundamentals. Elijah was a very successful professional basketball player in Germany during his playing years, and Tad had been a prosperous coach for many years for several NBA and Division I collegiate players. I really enjoyed playing for the Defenders, as it matured my basketball skills and gave me a new hobby outside of school. My teammates were great, and I had a successful playing career with the club team, which I thought really prepared me for high school basketball. I felt comfortable every time I stepped on that basketball court because I gained confidence in my abilities. I was also fortunate enough to play club basketball with one of my teammates, Isaac, who turned out to be one of my closest friends and still is to this day.

Eventually, I graduated from middle school in 2008. I had a relatively good middle school experience, but it was made better by playing for the Defenders on the side. During middle school and especially the summer before high school, basketball essentially became my life. It was all I thought about and cared about. I didn't focus on getting a girlfriend or anything like that. I fell in love with the sport and dreamed of playing in the NBA one day. I knew that it wouldn't just come easily, though. So I worked hard every single day, multiple times per day. I would work out with trainers, with my team, with friends, with my father, and by myself. If I had a basketball and a hoop at any given place, I would be on it. I was that kid who would be shooting hoops until one in the morning and have my mother come force me to go to sleep. That's how much it meant to me and how committed I was. I knew I wasn't the most naturally talented player, but I knew I had potential because I worked harder than any of my friends or classmates.

It was finally time for one of the most important experiences of my life to that point, which was the high school summer basketball tryout. It was the summer before my freshman year, and every person who wanted to try to make the basketball team was required to go through the summer program. I attended McKinney High School, and their basketball program put on a rigorous summer clinic to scout which incoming freshmen were good for the four rosters. Incoming freshman had the opportunity to make the freshman, sophomore, junior varsity, or varsity teams. The unlucky ones would end summer not on a roster. Workouts would be two hours per day and five days a week, with games or tournaments usually on the weekends. Going into the tryouts, I felt that my skills were polished and that I was going to be a good player and do well for myself.

As the summer program progressed, I showed signs of potential but didn't live up to the expectations I had for myself. I would often get nervous in practice, which resembled how I played back in elementary school with my friends. Something about the varsity coaches and players watching caused me pressure that I shouldn't have felt. I should have been able to just let my hard work and skills outweigh any extra distractions. But this wasn't the case. I would wake up each morning with a racing heartbeat because I was so nervous to walk on that campus to go to tryouts. It worked against me because I wasn't as aggressive and tended to be a little too tentative, if anything. I usually didn't make the most of my opportunities to impress the coaches, which was not a good sign. I was a very mediocre player in practice, but when it came to game time, I would get even more anxious. I wasn't much of a factor during games but somehow held my own throughout the stressful summer months.

By the time my freshman year of high school arrived, I found out that I had made the freshman basketball team. It could have been better by making junior varsity as a freshman, but I was still ecstatic to be on the team, especially considering that I knew I hadn't played as well as I could have.

Entering my freshman year of high school could not have had more positive signs. I was on the freshman basketball team, starting at a brand-new school, and meeting new people around campus. I met this girl named Sofia in an elective class. In the beginning I didn't know anything about this girl besides the fact that she had beautiful straight blond hair, glowing hazel eyes, and a warm smile.

Something about her just made me want to get to know her. She was one of those people whose good presence could be felt in the whole room no matter the situation. We would talk from time to time as the year progressed. She put a smile on my face every time I spoke with her. We became friends and grew much more comfortable with one another. We got to know what each other's interests were. She loved softball and aspired to play on the high school varsity team, just like I did for basketball. She was very nice and had a good sense of humor. I could tell that she had lots of close friends and was known by almost everyone. I was excited to find out about all these qualities. I definitely liked Sofia as a person and as a friend and started to develop some more feelings about her as our freshman year was coming to a close. I don't know how she felt about me, although there were signs that made it seem like she had mutual interest in me.

But as we grew closer, I found out that she had a boyfriend. His name was Jeff, and he was on the varsity football team. He was one of the star wide receivers. Jeff was also two years older than she was, so I knew I had no chance with Sofia, considering the combination of his age and him being on the football team, let alone the fact that they were already in a relationship. Oh, did I mention that he was six foot three? He made me look like a shrimp. During the year, I had met Jeff through Sofia many times. He seemed to be a nice guy but came across as a little conceited. I remember the football team doing well during my freshman year. That definitely worked in Jeff's favor and made him even more superior in her mind. But even still, something told me that Sofia might have had just the smallest amount of mutual interest in me, which was enough to keep me even more interested than I already was.

My freshman year of basketball was a learning experience. Our team had a brand-new coach by the name of Coach Dotkins. He was a tall, charming African American man and always walked around with a big smile. He played Division I college basketball back in the day. He was a great guy, and I enjoyed his presence on the basketball court. He was a wealth of knowledge and did a fantastic job in coaching us to get better as individuals and as a team. During some practices, he would have his kid race the team up and down the court. His kid was so fast that he would beat nearly everyone. Coach Dotkins used this as proof that we needed to get in better shape, and he definitely had a point. He was good at making the team build trust in one another. We didn't have a good season, ending the year with a losing record. But it could have been much worse. We still won some games and progressed as a team and had fun while doing so. I would sometimes play in the starting lineup and other times come off the bench. I wasn't one of the main contributors on the team, but I still got significant playing time and helped the team when I was on the court. I was a solid role player. My freshman year experience was good, but I was aspiring to move on to bigger and better things on junior varsity as a sophomore. I knew I wasn't good enough to make varsity quite just yet, but I sure as hell didn't want to play on the frosh team again because I viewed that as not being a step in the right direction.

When basketball season ended in February 2009, I didn't have much to do. I had no interests or hobbies because basketball was my only focus. All we would do in the offseason was show up for sixth period practice. Most of the time the coaches didn't even show up, so the players just waited around until the bell rang for us to go home for the day. When the coaches did occasionally show up, all we would do is shoot around or run some conditioning drills. I liked it because it was much less stressful, but I also despised the lack of competition. As a result, I naturally turned most of my attention to Sofia, even though she had Jeff. I would try to hang out with her every chance I could, whether it was in class, at lunch, or even watching the varsity basketball games. The thing that was cool about it was that she was always so excited and willing to hang out with me. It was mutual. Eventually, finals came around, which meant it was the end of my freshman year of high school. I was very excited for summer and to be able to get out of the classroom; however, I knew that I would be seeing much less of her over summer than I did every day at school. I knew that summer wasn't going to be all fun and games. My priority stayed on trying to make the junior varsity team while maintaining contact with Sofia.

2

Rocky Roads

Just like the previous summer, I would wake up every morning with nervousness that was difficult to withstand. I knew what was at stake for my basketball career. If I ended up making junior varsity, that would put me right where I wanted to be. But if frosh was calling my name again, I knew that would delay my progression to someday play varsity. Summer tryouts as a sophomore were even more stressful because I was now one year older, and the coaches expected more out of me. I had a very similar showing to that of the previous year. I didn't impress on the court as much as I would have liked, but I kept a good attitude and work ethic. The junior varsity coach's name was Coach Thomas, and I was doing everything I could to make him feel that I deserved a roster spot on his team. The summer was coming to a close. Basketball was brutal and had me burned out. I had only seen Sofia a couple times over the summer, since we were busy with our sports practices. So I wasn't necessarily opposed to the fact that school was starting again.

Just a few weeks into my sophomore year, I was notified that I had made the frosh team, not junior varsity. I was infuriated. I had talks with my family and friends every night about why I deserved to be on junior varsity and how I didn't think it was fair. I told them how skeptical I was of my playing career because I felt it was all becoming stagnant. My family has always been good at talking things out and making sure I carried a good attitude, so I eventually had to come to terms with it and try to make the most of the situation. Although I was disappointed to be left off the junior varsity roster, I didn't give up. I continued working hard every day in hopes that in the middle of the season Coach Thomas would bump me up to junior varsity.

By this time it was September 2009, and the freshman team had just been notified that Coach Dotkins had decided to leave the program because he and his family had moved. This surprised me, and I was sad to see him go, but I was hoping for a new coach just as good as he was. On the first day of practice, we met our coach for the frosh team. He was a guy by the name of Coach Norris. He was an older white man, who had an intimidating face, bushy hair, and he would walk around the gym with a smirk that couldn't be ignored. When one of the kids would say a joke, he would occasionally let open this big grin with an obnoxious laugh. But those laughs were rare. He was a very serious man. He forced our team to have practice every Saturday morning at six, which we all absolutely despised, since that was supposed to be our rest day. But I knew what I had to do, and that was to keep working hard and not complain about a damn thing.

As each practice and hard day of work went by, I started to become irritated with Coach Norris. One simple mistake and he would scream at the top of his lungs. His angry scream sounded like a dying animal. It was ferocious and bothersome. When the team would have a bad day of practice, he would make us all run nonstop for an hour. Players would be nearly keeling over, about to puke at the end of practice. I understood the concept of discipline and being physically fit, but the way he forced it excessively upon us was nearly unheard of. Well, at least I thought it was. But we all handled it and pushed through it to become better athletes.

But over time things were starting to add up. His brutal workouts, unnecessary screaming, and frequent insulting jokes began making me question his authority. The season dragged along slowly. Each day was terrible and the furthest thing from fun. I missed Coach Dotkins very much at this point. It was only December, and we weren't even into league play yet, and it was already an awful year. Our team was terrible, with a record of one win and eleven losses. I averaged just five minutes of playing time per game. I was not even one of the worst players, realistically around the middle of the pack as far as skill level. However, for some reason, he would rarely put me in the game. I showed up to every practice and treated every one like it was my last. Even if we were losing by thirty points, he would just play whomever he felt like, and that certainly wasn't me. I also remember seeing some of the parents go up and talk with him personally about their sons' playing time, which became a political contest. When this happened, the son of the parents usually began to receive more playing time. I told my parents to never intervene because I thought that wasn't the right thing to do, and that I would handle my own playing situation.

I was growing wildly frustrated with Coach Norris. Having him be rude and unfair was hard to deal with and made me unmotivated to want to take his coaching advice. I decided to talk to him one day after practice, and I stated everything that I was feeling. I told him that I did not appreciate how rude he was to the team while also excluding me personally from not playing much. I asked him why I wasn't getting any playing time, and he stood there with this startled look on his face and his mouth wide open, unable to answer. I told him that it didn't make sense to not try new rotations with the lineup, considering our awful record. If we were a great team with plenty of success, I wouldn't have been questioning him. But sitting on the bench as I watched each team we played destroy us was demoralizing.

As a result, the next three games, I surprisingly saw more playing time. He obeyed and honored our conversation. I was shocked that Coach Norris actually considered my initiative. We lost each of those games, but I played well, and at least held my own on the court. I was good enough to be out there on that court seeing playing time like the rest of the kids. But before I knew it, I was back on the bench with only five games left in the season.

Off the court, things with Sofia began to change. We had several classes together and would see each other every single day. By this point, we had become much closer and had gotten to know each other well. Every day in class she would give me compliments. She would say how she thought I was a nice, funny guy and whatnot. She frequently tried to entice me by saying that she "wanted a change, someone who is funny and with nice, blue eyes." Following that statement, she would instantly jump into saying how things were unstable with Jeff. She said that she didn't know if she loved him anymore and vice versa. All signals were pointing in my direction, and I loved that. We began hanging out together on weekends and everything. At this point, Sofia and Jeff decided to take an official break from each other. They would still casually hang out but not have the title of being in a relationship. I hadn't paid too much attention to Jeff when I had first met Sofia. But it was now at the point that I would become jealous if I ever saw them together. One of the reasons was because I desired to be with Sofia, but I also didn't like how she would say good things about me and then just give her affection right back to Jeff. It was easy for me to tell that Sofia was caught between knowing exactly what she wanted. But she loved the attention, especially from two different guys. I should have taken that as a sign from the beginning, but I decided to stay persistent with Sofia. I saw her as a beautiful girl with such an uplifting personality, so I wanted to give the situation a chance.

But as the year continued, I started to become very stressed out. The combination of Coach Norris and Sofia was a lot for a fifteen-year-old high school kid to deal with. I maintained my good grades in the classroom; however, my motivation was lacking. I would dread going to each class and sometimes would just even put my head down on the table during the entire class period. None of my friends understood that I was having a difficult time, and they would choose to laugh at me instead of trying to help me.

I never wanted to let my growing emotions show with my family in our house either, so I kept them to myself. I wanted my parents to think that I still liked high school and that basketball was going well. I was driven to make sure that I wasn't rubbing any negativity onto my little brother, Josh. He looks up to me as his big brother and best friend. But sometimes my head would become so overtaken by the stress that I would feel upset. It got to the point where I was walking around campus with a hood over my head, not wanting to talk to anyone. I completely stopped participating in class and kept my head down the whole time. When the teacher called on me, I just kept my head down and didn't answer the question. It started to feel like I was slipping into sadness, not just stress. I didn't talk to my friends as much, choosing to be alone instead. I started to feel depressed, angry, jealous, and frustrated by my coach excluding me and the uncertainty of the situation between Sofia and me.

It reached winter break, which meant that we were away from school for three straight weeks. Usually I love this time of year and spending Christmas and the holidays with my family. But this time around, I was not the same person. I had become so depressed over the past couple of months. Things were bleak and uninspiring. I lost motivation. It started feeling like true depression. During winter break, on Christmas Day and the next day, I slept in my bed for thirty-one hours straight. I only got up to use the bathroom. I had my mom bring me food because I didn't want to go downstairs and visit with the family. It was a dark holiday season for me. I couldn't even get out of bed. Thirty-one hours trapped under the sheets. Nothing seemed to be going right, except for one thing.

During the course of the year, I started growing very close with my German teacher, Ms. Reeves. The reason was far beyond the fact that she was a great teacher. She knew I was depressed, and she was one of the few people during this entire time to care to personally reach out to me. She would check up on me nearly every day to see how I was doing. One day, I was really upset, so we walked outside together and sat on a bench, away from the commotion and stress. We started talking about our lives. She shared some stories with me, and she looked me in the eyes and said to me that she knew exactly what I was feeling with this constant sadness. Ms. Reeves told me that she was depressed herself because there were problems in her marriage, among many other things. We spent nearly thirty minutes each day talking to each other during lunch break about what was going on. She tried to help me, and I tried to help her. Ms. Reeves was one of the few people who I felt sincere compassion from, which was reassuring. I felt that nobody else really cared. All people cared about was being the most popular and hanging out with the in crowd. That didn't sit well with me. But I truly enjoyed being around Ms. Reeves instead of my friends and classmates. She was the only person in my life who could actually relate to my situation, and I could do the same for her. Each day we built a stronger bond together, and she became one of the people who I was closest to at that point in time.

3

Check-In

In the middle of February 2010, we had reached the final game of the season, concluding my sophomore year on the basketball team. Our last game was against the best high school in our league. I was so ready for this game to be over so I could move on from this horrid season and the coach that I did not see eye to eye with. My frustration had carried on for almost the entire season, and it almost felt like I couldn't control it. There were ten minutes left in the game, and our team was losing by twenty-five points. Then an interesting idea popped into my head. I had completely stopped caring about this season, as it was disastrous in all facets.

So I decided that I would check myself into this game, since it was almost over and I had received no playing time. I was confident that I could get away with this without Coach Norris even realizing. He would get so wrapped up in the game that he wouldn't be aware of his surroundings. So I left the bench and ran right behind his legs to the scorer's table. I sat there patiently waiting for my opportunity to check myself into the game. I saw my teammates' faces, and they looked confused but excited for what I was doing. Eventually the whistle blew, and I entered the game. I lasted a solid three minutes on the court without Coach Norris even realizing that I had made a self-substitution to enter the game. He was still coaching but didn't even notice that I was on the court without his permission. But once he finally noticed I was out there, it went downhill quickly. He screamed at the top of his lungs, "Greg! Get your ass off that court and on this bench right now, kid!" I finished the current possession and obeyed him. I walked back to the bench, and he furiously stared me down, with words that made me nervous: "You and I are going to have a talk in the locker room afterward," he said.

The final horn sounded, and that concluded our atrocious season. We finished with three wins and twenty-one losses overall, and one win and nine losses in league play. We headed to the locker room with somber faces. During the final speech, my teammates and I expected him to say that he enjoyed coaching us, or something on a positive note, despite it being a rough season. However, he just went on this big rant on how we sucked as a team and should have won more games if we had played better and committed fewer turnovers. Within a minute, he turned his full attention to me. He approached me, looked me in the eyes, and said, "What in the hell did you just do out there, kid?"

"You clearly saw what I did," I responded. I told him that I decided to do that because I hardly played at all this season. I told him to his face that I was fed up with him. We started getting into a shouting match as my teammates stood to the side, speechless. Coach Norris and I were in each other's faces, screaming ferociously. When he would scream, spit uncontrollably came out of his mouth and splattered on my cheek. The two of us viciously exchanged curse words. I hadn't drunk my full bottle of water because I wasn't exhausted after sitting on the bench nearly all game. So I quickly walked a few feet to the right, reached into my bag, and there it was. I opened the cap in a split second and impulsively showered him with my entire water bottle, getting it all over his face and clothes. He was shocked and caught off guard. It took him a few seconds to process what actually happened. My teammates were at a loss for words, but they kept telling each of us to stay calm. He demanded for the entire team to leave the locker room, except for me. All fourteen other players exited the locker room. That left me, a furious kid who wanted to make a point, and Coach Norris, who was wiping his water-filled face off with a towel. He came up to me and put his face two inches away from mine. I could smell his bad breath and see his sweat mixed with the water that I poured on his face. He looked me in the eyes, and said, "Greg, if you ever do something like that to me again, you're going to be in big trouble, kid. You don't want to see what will happen. So cut the bullshit and get out of this locker room right now." I was sixteen at the time, and I freaked out. I broke down in the frustration and anxiety that I had been constantly feeling. I grabbed hold of his shirt, pushed him against the wall, and then stormed out of the locker room.

I started running. And running. And running. And running. All I wanted to do was to escape the stress and be by myself in an isolated place. My parents were waiting in the stands for me to come out of the locker room, totally unaware of what just happened. Instead, I sprinted out the back exit so that nobody could see or catch me. All I wanted was to be alone. I was running for twenty minutes before I heard sirens trailing behind me. Someone must have seen and found out. Someone must have called. It was the police. I kept running for as long as I could, but I was getting tired. I knew I was in trouble and couldn't escape them, so I stopped. Just as the police cars were approaching, I jumped in the street in front of a car. The car wasn't moving fast at all, maybe fifteen miles per hour, and came to an easy stop. If it were going faster, it would have hit me. I was so upset that I wanted the car to hit me. About thirty seconds later, two police officers bolted out of their cars and ran at me to secure control over me. They thought there was a possibility that I was having suicidal thoughts, so they took control of me by putting me in handcuffs. Eventually the crowd of players with their parents came. Among the crowd, I saw my parents and brother through the flashing lights of the police car. Coach Norris was nowhere to be found. The police talked to my parents and explained what they were about to tell me. My parents confirmed the decision. I was handcuffed and placed into the backseat of the police car. They said they were taking me to the nearest mental facility.

I got to the building, and they escorted me into the hospital in a stretcher, despite having no injuries or illness. The first thing I had to do was take off my clothes and change into a hospital gown. Then they proceeded to take my blood, which I despised. But I did the blood test, and the nurse showed me my room. The facility was a long wing of bare white walls. There were about ten rooms, with four people to a room. I was required to sleep next to three strangers. When I entered the room, the lights were off, and it gave off a creepy vibe. Two people were asleep, but the one guy next to me was still awake. We had a small conversation as I tried to seem as little nervous as possible. He seemed very sketchy as did all the patients there. He asked me the reason I was there. I told him that I was depressed and had an incident with a coach. Then I asked him the same question. His response sent chills down my spine: "I stabbed my uncle with a knife. He survived." I tried to hold myself together, but I was appalled. I simply told him that I hoped everything worked out, and that I'd see him when we woke up in the morning. I did not want to get into a long conversation with this guy because he seemed dangerous. My head hit the pillow of my bed for the night, and I said my prayers.

The staff woke us up the next morning with a loud scream, saying that breakfast was ready. I was confused and still trying to process in my mind what had actually happened the night before. It felt surreal that I was placed into a mental hospital. We went into the breakfast room and ate the meal, which consisted of runny eggs, stale cereal, and watered-down orange juice. I was looking around the room at the different patients. Hispanics and blacks heavily populated the facility. Everyone looked angry or depressed, and some just looked crazy. There were many drug addicts, sex addicts, and people involved with crime. I made sure to stick to myself and not say anything stupid, as I was intimidated. I tried making friends with the staff members since they were easier to converse with than the patients. I was in there for three short days, though it felt like an eternity. All we did was eat bland meals, play basketball, and do basic algebra for our school session. The doctors put me on antidepressants that I was to take for a while until they viewed me as stable.

My parents picked me up from the hospital. They were happy to see that I was safe and coming home. They heard from some of the parents of my teammates what happened between Coach Norris and myself. My parents were infuriated with his behavior and how he nearly threatened me. I explained that a lot of it I was at fault for too, for letting my emotions get the best of me and acting out at him. They understood. They knew we hadn't seen eye to eye all season and that he treated me poorly on a consistent basis. They disliked his demeanor and were saddened and frightened when they heard the details of what happened after our final game of the season. I apologized to them for causing a scene and creating stress for them and other people. They felt bad for what I had to go through but admitted that they were confused when I decided to check myself into the game. They couldn't believe what had happened.

I was happy to be out of the hospital and to be home with my family. Josh was only twelve years old at the time, so he didn't understand how I was feeling. He was glad to have me home with him, but he thought it was weird how I wasn't my usual happy self. I was more close-minded, sad, and ashamed. As I thought more and more about that night, I started feeling a sense of guilt and remorse. Although I despised my coach, I realized that I created stress on so many people and I shouldn't have made those decisions, especially trying to jump in front of a car. I was extremely upset in the moment and acted irrationally. The feeling of guilt just enhanced my developing depression though. I continued taking the medications as I was told to do, but I did not feel any better.

A few weeks later, I was called into the main office of the high school. I had no idea why. When I entered, I sat anxiously in the front room. The lady called my name to have me come back into the office to have a talk with me. She told me that the high school was aware of everything that happened. She told me that Coach Norris had permanently left the school. I was shocked. I wasn't even really happy or upset about it, just surprised. Coach Norris's departure was surprisingly significant, as he had coached McKinney High School for thirteen years.

The lady in the office also suggested that I seek counseling with the health services, but I declined. I didn't want the kids around the high school to find out about it because I knew that I would get made fun of. People had consistently tried verbally abusing me ever since elementary school, and I just tried to ignore it.

I started feeling so depressed that I didn't talk to anyone, not even Sofia. She would go out of her way to try to talk with me and help, and I usually was unresponsive. My motivation was declining. Sometimes I would be so upset that I would raise my hand in the middle of class and ask to go to the bathroom, not to use the bathroom but because I would break down in tears. I began hating myself and questioned what my purpose in life was. I felt that I had no good to bring to anybody, even my family. I completely shut down during the spring semester of sophomore year. I would put on a fake smile at home to mask the feelings of sadness from my parents and little brother. I was ashamed and did not want them to know or think worse of me. They didn't realize how depressed I really was. I did not want Josh to think of me as being a weak older brother. So I kept all my feelings inside as they continued building up.

Eventually, it was spring break. My family had a trip planned to San Francisco. We were going to have a nice getaway and go to the Golden Gate Bridge and Alcatraz and explore the city. We were gone for ten days. My family enjoyed themselves, and it was nice for them to relax. For me, I wanted to escape from some of the stress, but it didn't seem to help. I struggled emotionally over spring break. Sofia and I communicated with each other a little more over spring break than we had been. I tried to enjoy myself on the vacation but still remained very depressed, and I really missed seeing Sofia. We returned home on a Sunday afternoon, and I knew we had school the next day.

On that Sunday night, I started feeling really upset, even much more than usual. The constant buildup of stress and emotional discomfort was hard to bear for much longer. I decided to call Sofia on the phone late that night, around eleven. For the first time ever, I told her that I really, really liked her and wanted to be with her. I was hoping to get a response that would boost my morale, but what I received sent me crashing down instead. She responded by saying, "You're a great friend, but I don't like you in that same way." I completely lost it. I had a mental breakdown. Being a struggling sixteen-year-old kid, I just wanted to be liked by my peers, but I felt that nobody cared about me. My intention was that Sofia would show the same affection that I had for her. All I wanted was for her to like me. I hung up the phone and told her I would see her at school the next day.

My parents and brother were asleep. It was quiet and dark in our house. I locked myself in my room, trying not to let them hear me cry. My emotions were running wild, and I knew inside that I could no longer handle the anguish and the pain each and every day. I began contemplating suicide.

4

Tip Top

The minutes slowly ticked by, and I began deciding my fate. The decision of taking my own life had crossed my mind many times in those past months but in a much less intense way than it was at that point. The incident with the car after the basketball game a couple months prior was more a heat-of-the-moment, irrational decision than actually trying to take my own life with intention. But on that night in my room, I knew in my mind there was nothing else to live for. Having me in this world was pointless. I felt that nobody benefited from me, so I didn't want to continue causing people anguish. I started thinking about how I would do it. I first wrote up a note directly to Sofia saying how much I cared about her, how I hoped she had a great life, and that she deserved the best. I had biology class with her during period five, which went on between 1:00 and 2:00 p.m. The class happened to be in the tallest building on campus. It's three stories high.

My mom drove me to school that day. When she dropped me off, it was scary to think that this could be the last time I ever saw her. I told her I loved her. I carried the note to Sofia in my pocket so she couldn't see it. I pretended all was okay in front of my mom and the family. But as I exited the car, instantly seeing all the kids laughing and having fun together on campus made me jealous. I wanted that feeling of happiness and satisfaction so desperately but couldn't find it throughout that whole year.

I carried on with the day. Period one went by. Period two. Period three. And finally period four ended. Then the bell rang for lunch. I went and sat on a bench in a private, secluded spot by myself. I didn't meet with Ms. Reeves. I took out a piece of paper and a pen, and I wrote down the name of every person who had positively impacted my life at some point. That was in one pocket, the note to Sofia in the other. The bell rang. It was time for period five.

I walked up the steps of the three-story building to my classroom, since it was on the top level. I was anxious and breathing heavily. I entered the classroom from the back door and saw Sofia there with this big, glowing smile on her face and heard her contagious laugh. I figured that was the last time I would see her. My teacher started the lecture, and I grew more anxious. I started sweating and couldn't sit still. My heart was racing. I asked my teacher if I could go to the bathroom, and he excused me. I quickly walked out the door and looked over to the balcony. But I wasn't ready yet. I took a walk around campus for about ten minutes, trying to calm down. I finally returned to class with about thirty minutes left in the session. I was ready to make the decision. After sitting in my seat for another ten minutes and calming down, I stood up and walked a few feet to Sofia. I slid her the note under her desk, without her seeing it right away. Without telling the teacher or any classmates, I exited the classroom and walked outside. Surprisingly, nobody followed or questioned why I was leaving the classroom momentarily. The teacher kept lecturing, and the students kept listening to him. They probably figured that I had to go to the bathroom again or something.

I walked along the balcony, and I looked over the railing. All I saw was concrete at the bottom. I stood there for about a minute, and then I took my left leg and swung it over the railing, slowly followed by my right leg. I was over the railing, standing on a narrow platform that was about three inches wide, barely balancing. My body was fully exposed to falling, but my arms remained holding on to the railing from behind. At several points I would completely let my hands go and make myself vulnerable to falling three stories onto concrete, possibly to my death. Once my momentum brought me very close to losing balance and falling, my instincts told me to grab back onto the railing. It wasn't as easy as I originally had thought to just jump and get it over with. This mental dilemma happened for about five long minutes of going back and forth between jumping or staying on the edge. I will never forget what I saw below me.

During those five minutes, I saw three different kids who made eye contact with me while I was on the ledge. They continued walking effortlessly to their destination on ground level. They probably didn't understand what was happening, that a kid was actually standing on the ledge of a three-story building about to jump. But they did nothing. As I was there for more and more time, I began hyperventilating and grew extremely anxious. One jump stood between life and death. Suddenly, out of the corner of my eye, I saw someone turn the corner around the staircase. I heard, "Greg, no! Stop! Don't jump! Get the fuck off!"

His name was Jake. We were acquaintances, and I had been going to school with him since kindergarten. He bolted over to me, and before I knew it, he picked me up forcefully from behind and I was on the other side of the railing, back on the safe part of the balcony. I started flailing my arms and legs at him, yelling for him to get off me, as he had me pinned on the floor of the balcony. He tried to keep me locked in so I wouldn't jump off. People heard us yelling and fighting, and the entire third floor of the building came out of their classrooms. It went from just Jake and me to about a hundred people rushing out of their classrooms in a matter of seconds. Some people helped Jake contain me. I was trying to escape everyone because I wanted to end it all. But too many people were on top of me, which kept me helpless from escaping their grasp.

The security came over and bear-hugged me and walked me down the stairs to the base level of the school. I was put in a golf cart and driven away to one of the exit gates, where I saw two police cars waiting for me. I was hyperventilating. My mom was at home, my dad was at work, and Josh was at the middle school. They had no idea what was happening during all of this. Once the police cuffed me and put me in their car, I was rushed to the same hospital yet again.

The school called my parents just a few minutes later. When they received the news, they were distraught. No words can describe how my family felt. My brother was in shock and didn't quite understand that it was actually true. He knew what I had done, but it was hard for him to process that it was real, that his brother tried to take his life. He didn't really know any better, or how bad it could have been. It was hard for him to believe that I even tried something like that.

I entered the hospital and already knew what to expect since I had been there previously. I was stuck there for a week. I was such an emotional wreck that I didn't care about anything or anyone. I was selfish. My parents came to visit me each day and would bring me some of my favorite snacks. I barely talked with them though. They would sit there and try to pry words out of my mouth, and I was too upset to speak. I sat there helpless. I appreciated their support, but had no desire to talk to them. There were no words to describe the sadness that I was experiencing but enough to attempt to act on ending my own life. I was so depressed that my body and brain felt numb. It was an absolutely dominating depression at this point. Each day that went by felt like a week. I finally got dismissed from the hospital. The only major change that they made was increasing my dosage of antidepressant medications.

As soon as I got released from the facility, my parents and I met with the high school to discuss the plans for the near future. They concluded that it was best for me to be homeschooled for the remainder of the semester. This would mean that from April to June, I would be a full-time homeschooled student. When I was told of this news, I was infuriated. I didn't want to be homeschooled, and I felt like it would make me feel like even more of an outsider.

Those couple months were some of the most boring and slow-moving months I had experienced. All I did was meet with my homeschool teacher every day and then have family time. I started noticing that I was hanging out with my friends much less and hardly ever received contact from them. Sofia began to distance herself, along with my other classmates. Not only would I be unable to hang out with people at school, but I also found myself very rarely spending time with friends on the weekends. I grew stronger feelings of loneliness on top of already feeling severe depression.

5

Round Two

When the school year ended that June, concluding my sophomore year, McKinney High School notified my family and me that I essentially had one more chance to remain at the high school. After the incident with the coach and the car on the same night, and now the incident at the building, the administration was scared for my well-being. The high school was aware of the incident involving my coach, as well as the attempted suicide. I was told that if I was involved in one more significant event that I was going to be forced to transfer schools.

As the summer between my sophomore and junior year began, there was nothing exciting or new happening in my life. The trend of not hanging out with friends continued into the summer. I also started to see a trend of going long periods of time without seeing Sofia. We would still talk, but it was infrequent. I was not at all excited for this summer because of my lack of social activity and the fact that I had to try out for the junior varsity basketball team. Once again, it was five days a week during the large majority of the summer. I was so unmotivated that it was difficult for me to even want to show up to the gym to play ball. My self-esteem was at rock bottom, and I felt like I had nothing going for me, so going out and competing against talented players was a daunting task. I tried to give it my all in hopes of making the team. I figured that if I just worked my butt off and earned a spot on the roster, then things would be looking up because I would be on a basketball team that wasn't instructed by Coach Norris. I showed up to practice each and every day. I got invited to play in the tournament games on the weekends; however, I wouldn't play much. Throughout the summer, I saw no improvement in my depression circumstances. I was quiet, reclusive, and felt hopeless. I was trying to find something to drive me to increase my happiness and self-esteem but failed to find anything during that whole year. The person that made me feel the best was Ms. Reeves, but it wasn't enough to dramatically make a difference. Nothing was. I ground out the brutal summer months of basketball tryouts and limited encounters with friends. My family was stable and always loving, but unfortunately I took that for granted, being a sixteen-year-old boy.

As the summer approached its end, the junior varsity coach reached out to me, informing me that I was left off the roster. I was very upset and grew angry over the players who I thought were less deserving of a spot than I was. My official basketball career had ended. It was really hard to take and process this news into reality. Ever since I was a little kid, I had dreamed of playing varsity ball, and maybe one day in college or the pros. But my number-one dream was crushed. I felt deflated and worthless.

When my junior year began at McKinney, I noticed some big changes, as well as some similar trends from sophomore year. The biggest change was not being able to play competitive basketball again. This was a daily struggle for me. It ate away at me and bugged me constantly. I was very upset that I wasn't able to move up in the program and that my playing career had come to an end. However, one similarity that I saw was that I maintained close contact with Ms. Reeves, even after not seeing each other over summer. I wasn't in her class this semester, but we would meet up during lunch to sit down together and talk. This was my favorite part of the day because for once I didn't feel so alone.

The other similarity was that Sofia was in another science class of mine. It happened to be in the same building and on the same third floor. It was just a different type of science class with a different teacher.

In the first couple of weeks of the school year, I had multiple breakdowns each day. I put my head down in every single class, completely tuning out each teacher. I chose to hang out by myself, except for when Ms. Reeves and I would spend time together. By this time, I had come to the realization that I would never be able to have Sofia as my girlfriend. I felt empty and worthless all together.

In just the sixth week of my junior year, I decided that it was once again time for me to put an end to all the pain. It was a dark Monday night, and I was beginning to prepare my final note to the world. Once again, I wrote every person's name on the list that positively impacted my life. Some names had a small meaningful message as well. On that Tuesday morning, I woke up with the feeling of anxiety of hanging over the third-story ledge later that afternoon awaiting my destiny. My mom drove me to school, and I kissed her good-bye. Period one went by. Period two. Period three. And finally period four ended. The flashback was nearly identical. It was time for lunch, and once again, I was preparing myself for my decision to take my own life. But instead of sitting by myself like last time, I decided to pay a visit to someone during the lunch hour. It was Ms. Reeves. We had already been hanging out during lunch each day, so I didn't want to break that habit.

I told her I was extremely depressed and felt worthless and hopeless. That is all I felt inside. I felt no happiness or positivity. It was the worst feeling in the world, and I wanted it to go away after dealing with it for nearly an entire year. We talked and talked, and she told me how she had grown even more depressed herself. She told me that I was not alone, and that she knew exactly how I was feeling. When the bell rang, she told me to contact her if I needed anything, and I told her that I would see her later. I hugged her good-bye and made my way to science class, knowing deep down that maybe I would not see Ms. Reeves later.

I walked in and once again saw Sofia giggling with a charming smile. It felt like déjà vu, but not in a good way. Midway through the class session, I got up from my seat and handed Sofia the note. I walked out the door, stared into the distance, and slowly gathered myself. I climbed over the railing. Unlike the previous attempt, I was only on the ledge for just over one minute, contemplating life. Should I jump to end it all, or shouldn't I? Deep down inside I wanted to jump to end the anguish, but once again I couldn't do it. Before I knew it, a teacher was behind me screaming in desperation for help and ripping me off the railing from behind. Similar to the previous attempt, that one minute wasn't long enough for me to make the decision to jump off. The teacher put me in a headlock on the ground, and I was helpless. I tried to get out of it, but police officers were there in no time. I was in tears and was driven off the property. So many intense thoughts and emotions were rushing through my head. I felt an indescribable feeling of stress, and I felt distraught, ashamed, helpless, and jealous. I was hyperventilating in the police car, once again. This time I was off to a different mental facility, one that was known to be even more intense. I would stay there for a week.

As I sat inside the facility, I tried to put it into perspective that I had just tried to commit suicide for the second time in public on my high school campus. I knew that was horrible. I didn't do it because I knew it was horrible. I did it because I truly wanted to die and end my constant pain and struggle. I didn't want to live this life anymore. Life wasn't worth it to me. The benefit of living did not outweigh the depression that had taken me over. I was so upset that life wasn't even fun. I felt trapped. Each day was such a personal struggle, so I resorted to trying to take my own life. But I did this with the intention that people would give me attention, as that is one of the things that I wanted but I felt was nonexistent. I felt that every other kid was happy, well-liked, and finding success in high school, while I was just failing and living miserably. I felt that nobody liked me. I felt alone. Everyone just knew me as that depressed kid who tried to jump off the three-story building and got in a fight with his coach. Well, that and Greasy Greg.

On my final day at the visit to the hospital, my parents came to visit me and brought some staggering news with them. Such news that I had no idea was even an option. My mom, dad, and little brother knocked on my room in the hospital, and I opened up. I was excited to see them, and they were delighted to see me. By this point, my parents were so concerned and distraught over my well-being that they could no longer trust me. They had the fear always in their mind that at any given point, I might be considering taking my life. My parents and brother were deeply saddened and felt bad for me. They even felt helpless and so confused about what to do. My brother was confused because he just wanted his normal, fun, playful big brother back. But instead, I had turned into an unhappy, closed-off kid. My dad asked me what the first thing that I wanted was. My response was that I want to go back to McKinney to be back with Sofia. He turned at me and firmly said, "No, son, that is not happening. I think we're going to take a different route for you." The news I was about to hear put me in a state of shock and would ultimately turn out to be a huge decision. My dad looked at me and told me that they had decided to send me off to Idaho. I was stunned. I was sad, angry, and upset, but more so confused. I was just completely caught off guard and at a loss for words. It didn't feel real.

My parents broke down the scenario for me. They said that they as a family had decided to send me off to a residential therapeutic treatment center in Meridian, Idaho, for one whole year. The name of it was Key Ridge. They told me that I would go to school year round and would graduate one full year earlier than if I remained in a public school. I was being sent off to Key Ridge because I was incapable of being stable in a real high school environment. The treatment center dealt with struggling teens and put them in a stable, trusting environment where kids could work on personal development while continuing high school education. I was so depressed and such a serious threat to myself that a therapeutic institution would keep me secured and safe. My parents wouldn't have to worry about my safety, as Key Ridge was a locked-in campus. They told me that an escort was going to pick me up early the next morning to fly me out to Idaho. My mom brought me a giant suitcase of clothes that she packed from home before she came to visit me at the mental hospital. I went to sleep, with my parents and little brother sleeping in the pullout bed next to me. I grew deeply saddened knowing that I only had a few more hours left with my family. It felt surreal.

We woke up together to an alarm set for 6:30 a.m. My mom and dad were so upset but tried to put smiles on their faces. They believed that this could be a new beginning for me, even though they were about to not see their son for several months at a time. My brother was sad. He had a blank look on his face, knowing that he wouldn't be able to see his brother for quite some time. But he remained optimistic for me. Then there was me. I was more confused than ever before. Just the fact that my parents had decided to send me away to another state in hopes that I would improve as a person was a scary thought. I was nervous and anxious. The sadness that I was leaving my family started to sink in.

At 7:30 a.m., we got a phone call in the hospital room from the front desk of the facility. It was a lady calling to inform me that someone was outside waiting to pick me up. It all started to hit me. This was really happening. I was about to move to Idaho because of what I had done. My family walked me outside. I dragged my heavy suitcase across the floor and approached the man. He resembled an NFL linebacker. He was six foot four and had the physical composition and muscle of a body-builder. He looked intimidating as all hell. He reached out his hand and said, "Hi, Greg, my name is Mark. You're coming with me today. Say good-bye to your parents and brother. It's time to go." I hugged my mom, my dad, and Josh so tightly. I told them I loved them and that I was sorry. I took one last look over my shoulder and waved good-bye as I walked to the car, tears dripping down my cheeks. My mom was in tears, and my dad was trying to hold his own tears back. Twelve-year-old Josh just stood there with a blank, saddened look on his face, shocked that his big brother was being taken away from him. I hopped in Mark's truck and was off to the airport.

6

Approaching the New Home

When we were heading to the airport, Mark started talking to me about what was going on in my life and the reasons why I was going to Key Ridge. I told him that my parents and the school district thought it was best for me because of my actions in high school. Although intimidating at first, Mark turned out to be a nice guy. He knew that I was nervous because my whole life was about to change. He told me that I would be in good hands at Key Ridge. He said it was a beautiful campus with great staff and would be a new learning experience for me. I took his word for it. We finally boarded the plane and were off to Idaho. Once we arrived at the terminal, I grabbed my luggage, and we started walking to his van so he could drive us to Meridian.

It was about a forty-five-minute drive into Meridian, Idaho, from the airport. When we approached the campus, my heart was racing. I felt overwhelmed and scared. It was such a dramatic change, and I knew it was permanent for the coming year. There was no turning back. Mark pulled into the parking lot, and we got out of the car. The first thing we did was go to the administration office and get me checked me in.

The lady at the front desk asked me for my basic information. I told her the basics that she requested of me: "Greg Vogt. Sixteen years old. Hometown is Simi Valley,

California. Reason for my stay is attempted suicide and depression."

When we were finished handling the information forms at the administration office, Mark walked me to ICU, the intensive care unit. On my walk over, I was looking around. The campus was beautiful. The size of the property was similar to that of a normal public high school's, but the scenery was breathtaking. The campus was nestled in a valley surrounded in every direction by hills and mountains. The campus had lots of trees and greenery. At the front of campus, there was a giant rectangular row where all the cabins, or houses, were located. There were about eighteen cabins with roughly fifteen guys or girls to each one. To the left of the cabins was one of our schooling areas. It looked like a house itself but was five stories tall. Behind all the cabins stood another schooling area, which also housed the campus cafeteria. In the building next door, there were several basketball courts, indoor batting cages, a small fitness center, a small indoor soccer field, and a rock-climbing wall. Behind that building was where the outdoor basketball courts and giant field area were located. Other surrounding amenities on campus included an auditorium that held over five hundred people, a pool, a putting range, a movie theater, a volleyball court, an archery range, a horse stable, and a church. I was able to get a scope of the layout of campus as I first stepped foot on the property walking from the administration office to ICU.

On our walk over, I asked Mark why I was going to ICU. He said it was standard procedure for the staff to check me out and see the belongings I have. I didn't really know what to expect. When we entered ICU, it gave off the vibe of a jail or something. It was underground and consisted of no windows, or escape routes. The walls were white and had no pictures or anything. It was blank and eerie. When I walked in, I saw two things that caught my attention. To the right of me was a girl crying in a room curled up in a ball. In front of me stood a man much larger than Mark was. His name was Walter, and he was a large Samoan man who used to play on the offensive line for the Boise State football team many years ago. He called me over and took down my information on a piece of paper. He went through my belongings. I asked why he was doing that. He told me that it was required to search through each incoming person's luggage. On campus, these items were not permitted: phones, iPods and other electronics, weapons, sports team logos, skeleton symbols, possible gang attire, and all black clothes, among many more. The only electronic device permitted was an old-school transistor radio.

When he searched through my bag, he took some items out and created a pile of what was going to be sent back home to my parents. There wasn't much, but the main items were my phone and all my Los Angeles Lakers gear. I was appalled that the residents were not allowed to wear any sports team apparel. Once he finished going through my luggage, he took me into a private area of ICU. He opened up a curtain and said it was required for me to take off all my clothes to search my body fully naked for any gang-affiliated tattoos, piercings, or other markings. I felt pretty damn uncomfortable and violated, especially considering this was all within my first thirty minutes of ever stepping foot on the campus. If I decided to decline his request, I would have been forced to stay in ICU for a couple of days. That seemed beyond miserable, so I stripped off my clothes and got buck naked, and he observed my body for about five total seconds. It felt like a minute. I quickly put on my clothes again, exited the room, and gladly left ICU with Mark.

We were walking toward the row of houses. Mark looked at me and said, "Greg, here's your new home for the next year. You're in Timber, which is also known as Cabin One."

Each house was named after nature in Idaho, an animal, mountain range, river, tree, and so on. Each house name had a cabin number correlated to it. We walked up to the house. From the front view of the house, it was a fairly large two-story home. The front yard consisted of freshly cut grass and a nice, welcoming walkway up to the front porch. We walked up and knocked on the door. I was nervous to be forced into such an uncontrollable new situation. A man named Tom, who looked to be in his early thirties, greeted me first. "Welcome to Timber, Greg!" I put on a smile and said thank you and slowly walked in the door.

The scene that I saw inside that house was ridiculous. It resembled parts of *Cheaper by the Dozen*, where each kid was doing something totally different around the house. Timber was home to fifteen boys between the ages of fourteen and seventeen. When I stepped foot in the house, I was trying to absorb everything that I was seeing. There were two people arm wrestling in one corner, three people reading books on the couch, three people playing cards on the floor in front of me, one person drawing, two people listening to a transistor radio, three people playing guitar, and one person doing intense push-ups in the back corner by himself.

I felt overwhelmed and a little intimidated. I just walked in, hoping that someone would greet me, as these kids would be my housemates for the next 365 days. The first kid who came up to me was a guy by the name of Barry. He had stringy hair and was working on something that looked like a workbook of some sort. We began talking for a bit. He said how he was one of very few people at Key Ridge not from the states of California or Texas. He was from New Mexico. I learned quickly that a common question to ask new arrivals was, "Why are you here?" He asked me, and I simply told him for depression and suicidal actions. I asked him the same question, and he said the same exact thing but also added that he had a drug problem. He had already been at Key Ridge for one full year and had no indication of when he was going to be discharged from this residential treatment facility. He told me that a lot of Key Ridge kids were here for drugs and depression. Other common reasons included gang relations, serious family problems, violence, theft, anxiety, and more. I had a lone problem with depression, and nothing else. I had never done drugs, nor had family problems or joined a gang or anything. It was just the one thing. But it was a big one thing. Big enough to force me to try to take my own life and consequentially move states and spend the next year of my life at a rehabilitation center.

Once people saw Barry and I having a lengthy conversation on the back couch of the living room, more people began coming up to me and introducing themselves. There was a wide diversity in the races, ethnicities, and physical appearances of the guys in the house. I was trying to make a good impression and get more comfortable with my surroundings. Each guy that I met seemed nice and welcoming. We were able to hold casual conversations, which was helpful for me to get my mind off things. A guy in his mid twenties came up to me and pulled me aside. His name was Nolan, and he was one of the other primary staff members in Timber, along with Tom. Nolan was really nice and just told me that if I ever needed anything to feel free to come to him for whatever that might be.

In the first hour in Timber, I felt a lot of emotions. I felt sad because I was away from my family and away from home permanently. I felt overwhelmed by the adjustment that I was being forced into making. I felt somewhat intimidated by some of the guys that were around and having to face a major adjustment so fast. And lastly, I felt embarrassed. When the kids in Timber would ask me the stereotypical question of, "Why are you here, man? Why are you at Key Ridge?" I somberly responded by saying because of depression and attempted suicide. The reason I felt embarrassed was because of the common response I would receive. The kids would look at me and tell me that I'm stupid for doing that, stupid for believing that I am worthless enough to try to take my own life. They would follow that up by saying every person who attempts suicide is better and more worthy than that to take their own life. I had never really gotten that reaction before, so I felt humiliated at times. But it was also reassuring to hear that kind of positivity. Nobody at McKinney gave me that kind of support, except for Ms. Reeves and Sofia, at times.

As we all sat in the cafeteria for dinner, everyone was telling me how I came on a bad day. I was confused by what they meant. But since I arrived at Key Ridge on the evening of Halloween 2010, the guys would make jokes about how I couldn't wait another day to come. They were referencing how they would be out partying and celebrating if they weren't at Key Ridge and how I should be too.

Later in the evening, we returned to the house. Tom and Nolan ordered us to get ready and clean up the house.

Once we were finished, we headed upstairs to be in bed by our nightly bedtime of 9:45 p.m. I brought my big suitcase up the stairs and into my assigned room. The upstairs had one narrow, small hallway with just white walls and a carpet. On each side of the hallway stood two large rooms. There were four rooms upstairs in total, which held four beds each, making a total of sixteen spots. I was shown my room. We had bunk beds, so the room consisted of four major things: two sets of bunk beds, one bedroom window, one bathroom that the four roommates shared, and last but most important, one wall with pin tacks that we were allowed to post pictures of family and friends on.

I introduced myself to my three new roommates. Their names were Lance, Rafael, and Clark. Lance was an athletic, big guy who worked out a lot by doing push-ups and playing sports all the time. He had long, reddish hair that went down to his shoulders and a lot of freckles. He had a big crush on one of the girls on another unit. Rafael was of Indian descent and was pretty short. He liked to have conversations about anything really, and had a goofy side to him. Clark was really tall and kind of nerdy. He seemed like a very nice kid. Before our staff members told us to be quiet and turn off the lights for bed, I asked the three guys what a typical day looked like at Key Ridge. We would go on for thirty minutes talking about that before we fell asleep.

7

A Typical Day

"**E**verybody wake your butts up! It's time to get up for school!" Those were the first words that I heard on my first morning at Key Ridge. I checked the time on my clock beside my bed. It read 6:30 a.m. I was not a happy camper. The four of us had to arrange how we would go about our mornings. We had less than forty-five minutes to get ready as an entire cabin, and complete our required chores before the entire cabin left in a single file line to drop off our laundry, head to the medical station, and go to the cafeteria for breakfast before school. So one person in each room would shower while another person would do his hygiene. The other two people would gather up the dirty clothes and create a laundry pile for our bucket. We each were assigned individual chores for our rooms that we were to do each morning and night, such as scrubbing the toilet, cleaning the shower, being in charge of laundry, and cleaning the windows. When the shower was open, I took a quick five-minute shower, brushed my teeth, put in my contacts, and then did my chore for the week of cleaning the windows. Once the entire cabin was ready, we would all march down the stairs together.

We all walked in a single-file line, with Tom in front and Nolan in back. Each of us had our laundry buckets that we took to the community-style laundry room where we would pick it up for the day after school. We would stumble through the slushy snow and in the frigid weather, on bad days. Once our laundry was dropped off, we gathered in our single-file line and headed toward the medications station. This is where we would all wait in a small room and get called up one by one to take whichever meds we were prescribed. The nurse would give me my prescribed antidepressant medications with a small cup of water. I was required to take it right there in front of her. Once I swallowed the pills, she would shove a wooden stick under my tongue and all over my mouth to make sure that I wasn't trying to hide the pills and fake swallowing the meds. Some kids would try to do that in order to crush the pills and snort them later on. That never crossed my mind, but I soon realized that was a common thing among the kids, along with some other rebellious actions. They would never get away with it though. I took my meds, sat back down, and waited for the rest of the guys to take theirs.

Once we had finished, we lined up and marched toward the cafeteria. Breakfast was at 7:30 a.m. each morning, and we would eat in the large cafeteria room along with the other cabins that housed males. The female units were never with us in any activities, as we were prohibited from interaction with the opposite sex. We lined up at the cafeteria and waited our turn to get our food. Surprisingly, the food wasn't atrocious. I thought it was going to be mushy, disgusting food for an entire year, but it wasn't that bad. I actually thought it was pretty good. Even if the line was long and we didn't sit down until later to eat our food, we were still forced to leave the cafeteria to be at school on time by 8:00 a.m. That meant you either ate your food as quickly as you could, or you could have just not eaten, if you hadn't already consumed your meal.

We walked together in a single-file line to one of the school buildings. Everywhere we went, we walked in a single-file line. The boys were always in one building while the girls were in another. Boys and girls were never allowed to be in the same room during any activities. When we walked into the school, I approached the front desk and received my schedule. Most of my classes were general education classes like math, science, history, etc. I really had to get used to this whole school routine, because Key Ridge was a year-round school.

On my first day of class, I realized that most of my teachers were really nice and willing to help. They understood that most of their students were not fully focused on school, instead focused on getting their lives back on track. In each of my classes, I tried making friends with some of the new guys in other cabins. Even though most of the kids weren't in my cabin, Key Ridge was such a small school that I would be interacting with these people at length on a daily basis, especially because we were not allowed to talk to girls. School lasted from 8:00 a.m. to 3:00 p.m., Monday through Friday each week. We would go to three classes in the morning and then we had an hour lunch break from 12:30 to 1:30. Timber would meet outside and enter the cafeteria to eat lunch together.

Once we finished lunch, we had the opportunity to do a few different things before our next class session. We could stay and talk with staff members, work on homework, or go to the basketball court to play some hoops. I played basketball every day. At this point in my life, I was still upset about how Coach Norris dampened my enjoyment of the game, so I used this opportunity to regain the fun of the sport. Some of the best players at the school would gather and either play full-court pickup games, or we would just shoot around. I always participated in this and enjoyed the physical activity.

I learned very quickly that, ironically, the best basketball player at Key Ridge was in my cabin. His name was Peyton, and his father played several seasons in the NBA. Peyton was a tiny, five-foot-three point guard, but was quicker and more athletic than anyone else. He was so athletically gifted that at the age of sixteen, he was able to jump and hang on a ten-foot rim, even as small as he was. Lunchtime was usually good because it was a nice break from school and allowed all the kids to play basketball together. Once the bell rang, we would gather our backpacks and head to our final two periods. After the school day ended, we would pick up our laundry and then head back to Timber. From 3:00 to 4:00 was our homework time. We were instructed to work on any assignments or studying we had to do. If we had no schoolwork, we were required to work in our workbooks. We were not allowed to talk during this time.

Every person on campus was given a workbook by his or her assigned therapist. Each kid had a therapist that they saw a couple times a week to work on improving on a personal level. Although it doesn't sound like much, the workbook was a really big deal. The workbook consisted of hundreds of different tasks and goals that the individual had to work toward and accomplish. Once a task was finished, I would get it approved by my therapist so I could move on to the next one. There were a couple of main reasons the workbook was important.

First, it was designed to help each kid on a personal level. If you were willing to put in the work to accomplish the tasks, then it would only be beneficial going forward. Some tasks were basic, like making one new friend that week or getting all your schoolwork in on time. But other tasks were more complicated, such as learning techniques to cope with my depression. Parts of the workbook were standard for every person, while other parts were custom-ized tasks based on the problems that person was facing in his or her life that contributed to why he or she was at Key Ridge.

The second main reason the workbook was important was because the more that you accomplished, the likelier you were to move up the number system. Key Ridge had a system where the incoming kids were categorized at level 1. With this being the lowest level, you essentially had very limited freedom to do what you wanted. There were levels ranging from 1 to 5. The harder you worked on improving yourself, and if your therapist trusted you, then the higher you moved up. As you moved up the level scale, you got certain privileges that were not attainable on the previous level.

At level 5, you could have an iPod, an on-campus paid job, and the access of actually going over to one of the girls' cabins and hanging out with them for one hour each week, among several more benefits. On level 4, you were allowed to go on the weekly off-campus events, including movies, restaurants, arcades, sporting events, and so on. On level 3, you were allowed to control the remote and channels of the house television during the permitted tele-vision hours. As a house, we were only allowed to watch television for a few hours per week, so it was common to access the remote on Sundays when NFL games were playing. On level 2, you gained access to have money added to your personal account so you could buy treats and snacks at the campus store once a week. And again, level 1 was essentially nothing, and you just tried to work your way up.

For these reasons, along with personal growth, it was evident from the start how important the workbook was to the program at Key Ridge. So if you didn't have schoolwork during homework time, then you were highly encouraged to work in your workbook. For the people that were lazy and unproductive, they would fake as if they were working in their workbooks, even when they wouldn't be. When it came down to it, each person would leave Key Ridge permanently in the future under two circumstances. The first option was finishing all required credits and graduating high school. But if you were very young and not close to graduation, the only other option for leaving was being discharged. What being discharged entailed was proving to yourself, your therapist, and your family that you were able to go home and live responsibly and safely in the real world. So it was really important to progress in the workbook in order to increase the chances of being discharged sooner, especially if graduation was not in the foreseeable future for a particular individual.

Once homework time was over, the entire cabin would head to a certain part of campus for recreational therapy. What this entailed was overcoming a difficult physical task as a group and then reflecting about what that could mean in life with our recreational therapist. I actually enjoyed this time of day a lot because most of the activities were fun. Once a week, we would have group therapy, which was similar to personal therapy. Following the recreational therapy each day, we would head to the cafeteria for dinner, and we were permitted one hour of gym time afterward. Similar to lunchtime, we would play a lot of basketball. We also had the option to rock climb, play soccer, or hit in the batting cages. After that, we headed back to Timber for a relaxation period, which was more personal time, from 6:30 to 8:00 p.m. During this time, we could do any activity around the house, like push-ups, playing cards, arm wrestling, homework, drawing, listening to your personal radio with headphones, reading, or writing.

After this session, the staff members would bring us an evening snack. It would usually just be a granola bar, a fruit cup, or applesauce, but on the rare occasions that we were brought Nutella and peanut butter sandwiches, it was like a celebration of joy. Even more rarely, we were brought a slice of chocolate cake, which made us feel like we won the Super Bowl. After snack time, we walked over to the med station and took our medications one by one. We walked back to Timber, and then our staff members would instruct us to clean up the cabin and do our chores. Such house chores included trash duty, mopping, vacuuming, cleaning bathrooms, cleaning the communal shoe room, wiping windows, porch maintenance, and many more things.

Chores were a very big deal at Key Ridge because each cabin would be inspected each week. If we got a perfect score on our cleaning for the week, we would be rewarded as a house by having more television time and more outdoor porch activities like throwing a football around. I know that sounds odd, but we were not even allowed to go in our own front yard, even just to catch fresh air or throw a ball around without supervision. The reason for this was because kids were known to use this as an opportunity to go AWOL, which means escape from the facility without anyone knowing. So the porch was a possible escape route for someone left unattended outside. But if we scored poorly on our chores, we would have to suffer through no television for the entire week and other consequences like that. So finally, once our chores were done for the night, we headed upstairs, brushed our teeth, and said good-night, only waiting for that loud scream waking us up for school at 6:30 a.m. the next morning.

8

The Big Boys

On my second day, I met some very important staff members on the Key Ridge campus. I got called out of my English class to go have a meeting with my academic advisor for the first time. He was an older man named Harold, and I soon realized he was one of the most kind-hearted individuals I have ever known. He would put a smile on every person's face that he ran into because of his everlasting charm. Harold and I were discussing the plan for my year at Key Ridge and what classes I would need to take to be on track to graduate. He then asked me if I knew who Brett was, and I responded by saying that I had never heard of Brett before. Harold said I would be introduced to Brett later that day and that I would be in good hands.

I got a call in the middle of period five because it was time for my "therapy session." I got to be excused from class, which was pretty neat. I was shown the office for therapy and walked in, and there I saw him.

"Hi, Greg! It's a pleasure meeting you. My name is Brett, and I will be working with you as your designated therapist during your stay at Key Ridge." He seemed really nice and genuine. I was willing to have an open mind, despite not being the biggest advocate of therapy, even when I really needed it during my most depressed times.

We began talking, and it lasted for an hour. We talked

about how I was feeling, my family, friends, the adjustment to Key Ridge and Timber, my depression, and where we would go from there. Brett told me how we would meet once each week to reflect on how things were going and also to improve upon something and set a goal. A lot of kids at Key Ridge ended up disliking their therapist due to personality conflicts, but I realized that over time, Brett and I tended to see eye to eye. He knew that coming into Key Ridge, I was unstable and suicidal, so he made sure that I had a gradual transition to the new lifestyle.

He reiterated how important the workbook was so I could move up in levels and to improve myself on a personal level. Another benefit of progressing as an individual and through the workbook was that if Brett noticed significant improvements, he would feel comfortable letting me take visits back home to see my family. Usually, kids at Key Ridge would go months at a time without seeing their families. For starters, we were only allowed one phone call per week for twenty minutes. So yeah, being homesick was often prevalent. But if someone were making minor improvements, the therapist would usually allow the family to come out to Idaho to see their kid and take them on off-campus visits in Meridian. And over time, if significant progress and trust by the individual had been made, the therapist would allow the student to fly home for about a week to see his or her family.

I noticed that Harold was right about how I would be in good hands with Brett. Although many people acted as influences, usually none were as important as the student's therapist. Later that afternoon when I returned to Timber, Tom and Nolan were not there. Instead, it was two other staff members by the names of Owen and Mike. Similar to Tom and Nolan, these two guys seemed to be in their twenties or thirties, and seemed really down to earth. I would grow really close to each one of these staff members throughout my stay. One last man who I met that day went by the name of Bart. He was this big guy and walked around campus with a presence that couldn't go unfelt. Bart was the main guy who managed all the staff members on campus. He would go over to each cabin and spend time with the staff and residents to see how everyone was doing. He was a great man, but if anyone ever got into trouble (which happened a few times per day), Bart would be the first one you would have to explain the situation to. He had a tough job, as he had to try to keep the kids happy and safe while also making sure the staff was in a good state of mind. There were about 250 kids on campus, and each day he would have to deal with incidents, including fights, AWOLs, thefts, and suicidal thoughts from students, to name a few. I gained a lot of respect for Bart and the supporting staff members in a short amount of time.

9

The Realization

Each day at Key Ridge was a difficult one. I essentially felt stuck on a campus that I could not leave and had very limited freedom to do what I wanted. I could not see family or friends from back home. I couldn't even call my family or text them, outside of my one twenty-minute phone call per week. I had no car or access to any electronics. I could not get alone time, even if I wanted, because we were forced to do everything together as a cabin. The adjustment to this lifestyle was indescribable and very difficult. Some people would go crazy, literally. So crazy that they would go AWOL to the nearest escape route or river, only to be caught by police later on and sent back to Key Ridge … in ICU. Some people would try to go AWOL on their visits back home but would eventually be caught by someone, usually family members. Not only would those students be back on campus but they would also be in ICU for a while and would drop levels. Yes, that was a major consequence. For example, if you were a level 5 and made a poor decision, then you could drop all the way down to level 2 or even level 1 and lose nearly all privileges and rewards you had.

Despite all the constraints and dramatic changes that Key Ridge proposed, I had to make a decision for myself: I could keep dwelling on the past and hope that people would feel sorry for me. I could stay in my depression that had taken over who I really was as a person. I could make my stay at Key Ridge miserable and not make any new friends or good experiences. I could create more despair on my family back home, only wishing that their son was safe and okay. I could continue to cause my family constant stress, concern, and loss of sleep.

Or, I could realize the new situation that I was put into and do something about it. I could use the great resources I had, including my therapist and staff leaders, and make new friends. I could work hard in school and in my workbook to improve as an individual. I could do the little, good things that would put my parents more at ease so they wouldn't lose sleep at night about the possibility that their son was still suicidal. I could change the selfish habits I had in high school and turn them into caring and selfless traits. I could be a better big brother, a better friend. I could take it in stride how we weren't allowed to converse with girls. Instead of hanging my head on that, I had the opportunity to take a different perspective that it was probably in my best interest to not engage with girls. Since this was an unstable stage in my life anyway, I could work on improving myself first before building relations with females. But most importantly, I could admit what I was doing wrong, take ownership, and make an action plan on how to change.

This realization did not hit me overnight. It took about a month for it to sink in. Even when I realized what options I had, it was still hard for me to actually act on my thoughts to make improvements. I was such a lifeless and self-conscious individual that it took so much to motivate me to even do the smallest of things. I wasn't confident that the people in Timber would like me or that I would do well in school or even that I could beat someone in a friendly game of one-on-one basketball. I believed I was the worst, that I had nothing to offer people and was undeserving of a good life. And those feelings contributed to why I chose to attempt to take my own life multiple times back at my old high school.

But as the first several weeks of Key Ridge passed, my mind-set began to open up. I began to realize all the pain I caused my family and how selfish I really was. I would literally sit on the couch in the living room of Timber, and my mind would just race. I felt so much guilt and remorse. I felt like a screw-up, a selfish bitch. It sank in that choosing suicide was a consequential and selfish decision, despite my unbearable depression. So I started to make little changes. I worked consistently in my workbook, studied in school, and tried to turn my pessimistic state of mind into a more positive outlook. It took the guidance from my therapist and others, but I knew that it was up to me in the end to make the necessary changes.

Despite the conflict of trying to fight my way out of depression and low self-confidence, one particular day provided me with a spark and shined hope into my mind.

On the second weekend at the school, Tom came up to me and explained how sports seasons usually go on campus. Out of all our staff members, he and Mike were by far the biggest fanatics of sports, which I loved. Tom was telling me how there are four sports seasons: football, basketball, soccer, and softball. Each season lasted a couple of months. The way it worked is that each cabin would have a team and play the team from every other male unit. Once the season wrapped up, playoffs would happen, concluding with the championship game. Tom told me that I missed the entire football season, as it went from September to the first week of November, but he said the championship game was that Saturday. That Saturday marked my second weekend of being on campus. Tom said that I was in luck because Timber was in the championship game against Cabin 8. I learned quickly that our house, Cabin 1 (Timber) and Cabin 8 (Crevice) both consistently dominated the sports on campus. I asked if I could play, and Tom emphatically said yes.

I had never really played an organized game of football before, with referees and everything. The furthest I had gone before that point was playing football for fun with friends. But I was excited to give it a chance. We had a couple days of practice out on the fields before game day, so we could prepare for the championship game against Cabin 8.

We woke up Saturday morning bright and early. The entire house was hyped and ready to take the field. We had our pregame meal at breakfast and focused on our strategy for the game. Tom and Mike knew a lot about football, so they were our coaches and instructed the team on what to do. After breakfast, we went back to Timber to get ready and grab what we needed for the game. I noticed that everyone had cleats, but I didn't have any since I was so new to campus.

Lance said he had an extra pair. "Greg, what size cleats do you wear?" he asked.

I said, "I usually wear like an eleven."

"Well, man, you're out of luck. You're wearing these cleats—size fourteen."

He tossed me them and I put them on. I laced them up as tightly as I could to see if it would make more sense to wear giant cleats or just go back to normal running shoes. I made the decision that I would go with the cleats. Surprisingly, the size fourteen cleats weren't even that big on my feet. They would have to do. We all walked over to the field together with an intimidating focus. The headphones were in our ears, and the mentality was to win. The two units had a history of getting into some feisty battles when it came to playing one another in big sports games. When we approached the field, I was surprised to see what awaited us. The entire school—boys and girls—were there in attendance. I didn't understand that it was that big of a deal and taken so seriously, until then. It was treated like a real championship game. The captains went out and did the coin flip while the rest of us were warming up to pumped-up music. Girls made signs and cheered for whichever cabin they wanted to win. Maybe the craziest thing of all was that the game was a snow bowl. It was snowing outside, and we had to play in the snow, with brisk, frigid winds. The audience kept warm with blankets, heavy coats, and hot chocolate. I was there wearing a light jersey, shorts, my flags, and my size-fourteen cleats.

When we were set to take the field, I was pretty damn nervous. This was my first real organized football game. And I was playing in a championship game … in the snow. I had the entire school and staff watching me. Since I had only been at Key Ridge for a week and a half, everyone picked me out like a sore thumb because nobody knew who I was, except for Timber and a few staff members. "Hey, who is that new kid?" I often heard people mumble under their breath.

Cabin 8 won the coin toss and selected to kick. We would receive first. I knew that our best player was Peyton, the short athletic kid. He was faster than lightning and could beat anybody with his quickness and athleticism alone. Lance and a guy named Adam were also good players. Peyton was our quarterback, despite being five three. He had a strong arm on him and could scramble out of the pocket if need be. I was one of the starting wide receivers and also played cornerback on defense.

At the end of the first quarter, it was all tied up, 10–10. I had one reception for about twelve yards. On the sidelines we had to keep warm, as it was a frigid twenty-nine degrees and snowing outside. Catching the ball without gloves was brutally difficult and would sting our hands, but we knew we had to push through it. We wanted to be the big dogs on campus.

The second quarter was underway, and the score remained even. By halftime, Timber was leading Cabin 8 by a score of 21–17. The third quarter saw the intensity and aggression rise. Peyton was doing most of the work for us. He had two passing touchdowns, one a piece to Lance and Adam. Peyton also had one rushing touchdown of thirty yards. Peyton was by far the best player on our team. A guy by the name of Reece was the best player on the opposing team. Reece was six three and had freakish length and athletic abilities. He could do it all, just like our star player. Reece would switch off between quarterback and wide receiver.

One play in the middle of the third quarter, Reece went long for a Hail Mary, as we were on defense. The quarterback launched the ball deep into the air, and there was Peyton, eyeing it down to break up the pass with his incredible leaping ability. When Reece went up to grab the ball in the end zone, Peyton trucked him from behind, not really making a play on the ball. Reece fell hard onto the icy grass and got back up in a fierce and quick way. He approached Peyton and went up into his face and started cussing him out, saying that was not okay to do in flag football. The referees sprinted over and broke up the altercation, knowing that fights happen frequently on campus. The referee declared the play pass interference and an automatic first down. He also gave Peyton a warning, which meant if something like that happened again, then he would be ejected from the game. Cabin 8 would go on to score on that drive, making it 27–21, as they had previously got a field goal earlier in the quarter.

There were just three minutes left in the third quarter, and we felt momentum start to change in favor of the opponent. We knew this was a dangerous point in the game and that we had to change the momentum back toward our team. We began the drive with a fifteen-yard pass completion to Lance. Then Peyton broke loose for a long, vicious, forty-yard run down the left sideline. We were fifteen yards out from scoring and taking the lead. He drew up a play for me to do a slant route across the right side of the end zone. The ball was hiked, and I started sprinting. I got separation from my defender, and Peyton lobbed the ball up, right into my arms. The referee yelled, "Touchdown!" I spiked the ball in enthusiasm and chest-bumped Peyton in the end zone. Hearing the cheers from the crowd was special. It was 28–27 in our favor, as the game entered the fourth quarter.

On the opening drive of the final quarter, Cabin 8 was just twenty yards away from scoring another touchdown. They hiked the ball on third down and threw it to the end zone, only to be intercepted by Adam. That was a huge stop for us, as we had possession of the ball now and stopped them from taking another lead. The weather really started to get worse, with a substantial downfall of snow. It was making it difficult to pass, catch, and even run. We couldn't really get an offense going on that drive and were forced to punt. Cabin 8 received our punt and had a good return of twenty-five yards. They went on to kick a field goal that drive, giving them a lead of two points with about five minutes left in the championship game. Peyton returned the kickoff for our team for just ten yards, as he slipped in the snow near the out-of-bounds line. We were down and just had a few minutes left to save our season. Peyton put together a few short passes in a row, one to Adam, and one a piece to two other guys who didn't play much. We were about fifty yards out from the end zone still. It was third down, and Peyton drew up a particular play for Lance, Adam, and I. We needed a first down to keep our hopes alive. It was a "trips" set on the left side. Adam was to shoot down deep the left sideline. Lance was to do a slant middle route and then head toward the left sideline. And my route was to do a quick jab left and then sprint deep toward the middle right side of the field.

He hiked the ball with just under three minutes to play. We all knew that one play or one turnover could end everything. We hit the ground running. Before he drew up the play, I thought he was going to throw it to Adam deep down the left sideline, as he was one of his most trusted receivers. But as I was running my route, I saw the ball in the air coming my way. I was really deep and only had one safety near me. He placed the ball real far out in front of me. I dove face first for the ball and slid five feet across the slushy ice near the out-of-bounds line. My feet were in, and the ball was in my hands. The crowd went crazy. I had just made a forty-yard diving catch in the snow to give our team the opportunity to take the lead. I was downed before the end zone, so we still had eight yards to score a touchdown. But I remember people screaming on the sidelines, "No way! How did he catch that? Who even is that kid?" The offense quickly ran up to the line of scrimmage, and we hiked the ball. Peyton faked a crossing route pass to Lance and instead took off with his speedy feet diving over the end zone. It was a touchdown! We took a five-point lead with just a minute and a half left in the game.

We just needed to stop them on four downs, and then we would be champions of that football season for Key Ridge. Cabin 8 started from the opposite twenty-yard line, so they had a long way to go. On first down, Reece used his giant legs and quickness to break loose for a thirty-yard run, getting his team to the fifty-yard line. The next two passes went incomplete. It was third down with about one minute remaining. Reece found a receiver in the middle of the field for a fifteen-yard gain, giving them the first down. They rushed up to the line. They were nervous. We were nervous. The crowd was nervous. I was especially nervous because I was playing cornerback and had to make sure the receiver I was guarding didn't break loose for a reception or a touchdown. They drew up an end-around running play for Reece to be handed the ball and run down the sideline where I was. When he was coming at me, I squared up, and snagged his flags before he could break loose for a touchdown. It was another first down, advancing them to the twenty-five-yard line with forty-five seconds left. He hiked the ball, threw it to the left corner, and placed it perfectly in his receiver's hands. It was a touchdown, and the crowd went wild once again, except not in our favor. They took the lead of 37–35 with thirty seconds left.

We took a timeout to discuss the game plan. Every down from then on, each receiver was going long, except for one staying short just in case Peyton was about to get sacked. Peyton returned the kickoff thirty yards, giving us a total of twenty-three seconds to work with. On first down, he threw a Hail Mary to Adam that was broken up and nearly intercepted by Reece. On second down, Peyton made a fifteen-yard pass completion to Clark on the right sideline. There were fourteen seconds left with fifty-five yards to go. Peyton quickly passed to Rafael for another twenty yards, and he barely got out of bounds to stop the clock from running down. We had no more timeouts left. It was the final play of the game. We were thirty-five yards away from scoring, and had seven precious seconds remaining in the game. The longest Peyton was able to throw was about forty-five yards, so we were fortunate to be in his throwing range. He hiked the ball. Cabin 8 placed all their defenders as safeties, so Peyton had an eternity to throw the ball. He launched up the Hail Mary into a big crowd of players of both teams. It was up for grabs. Our tallest receiver, Lance, went up to snatch the ball out of the air. It was inches away from his hands, and Lance's eyes grew very large.

Boom! Reece came out of nowhere and knocked the ball fiercely to the ground. It smacked against the chilly grass. That was it. Game over. Our team laid there on the cold, icy surface in disappointment and exhaustion. The crowd was a mix of cheers and groans. Cabin 8 was declared champions of the football season, as they beat us 37–35 in the championship game. We were devastated and angry, especially because we had just lost a heart-breaking game to our rival opponent, ending our season.

As we walked off the field with our heads hanging low, our coaches and staff members came up to us for a team meeting and told us how well we played and how proud of us they were. It was a frustrating ending for us all. That was my first game ever, so it was quite the experience. As I walked off the field with a wet shirt, frigid hands, and snow all over my body, many people I did not even know came up to me. Some were staff members, some were guys on other units, and a few were even girls … even though they technically weren't allowed to talk to me. They all introduced themselves and said how well I played, and told me that the diving catch I made was awesome. I quietly thanked them and told them it was nice meeting them. But I wasn't in the mood to talk.

A few days passed. Because Key Ridge was such a small campus, news traveled quickly. I had random people coming up to me saying that they heard about the catch I made in the final game. It made me feel pretty good that I was being recognized for something good that I did.

I remember sitting on the living room couch in Timber one week later. I was listening to my transistor radio with my headphones in. I was by myself, and I began thinking and reflecting. I realized that people were sincerely excited about the big catch I made in that football game the week prior. It seemed like such a good feeling that I had never really felt since my depression first began my sophomore year in high school.

For the past year, I had been putting up with Coach Norris degrading me and diminishing my love and passion for basketball. I had to deal with not being able to be with the girl I wanted to be with. I had to deal with constant verbal bullying from elementary school through high school. I had to put on a fake face during high school to hide my depression so that I wouldn't get bullied and made fun of more than I already had experienced. During this time, I had lost my identity of who I really was as a person and who I wanted to be. I had let other people take over my life and ruin the happy person that I once was and later envisioned being.

But as I sat there on the couch in Timber, I saw that catch I had just made as an opportunity. Even though it was just one catch in a school game of flag football, what if I used this to help bring back the confidence and positivity in my life? I needed something to change, anything really, because I had not felt true happiness in over one full year. That is too long for any person to go being unhappy.

At that point in my life, it was nearly impossible for me to tell myself that I was doing something good. I didn't think I deserved to be living, nor did I want to. So hearing other people actually mention my name in a positive manner felt out of the ordinary. Even during school the following week, people would come up to me congratulating me on "the big catch," despite Timber not prevailing in the victory at the end. But this is what I needed. It made me feel happy to know that people were recognizing me in good regards. I felt appreciated for once.

For the next two weeks, I noticed myself being more engaged. I was trying to be happier and not let my depression control me, though it was never easy. I worked hard in school and in my workbook. I kept trying to meet new friends and pick up new activities and hobbies. When my parents found out about this on our phone call that week, they were relieved and happy. They were proud that I had had an effect on the game. During therapy that week, Brett even said how he heard about my catch, and he said it was awesome to hear how I helped impact the game.

Inside Timber, we had a giant board in our living room. The board consisted of three things: each person's name, their weekly chore, and the level that they were currently at. In just my fourth week, I had reached level 3. During my weekly therapy session of my fifth week at the school, Brett and I began discussing the progress I was making. He was cautiously optimistic because he saw two sides in me. One was the emotionally torn side. But he told me he saw something else in me. He said that I had so much potential to change my life, even though that was far from the case, due to my current state of mind. He said we needed to work together to break through the barrier of my depression that was so hard to overcome. But he was telling me that he was so impressed with how hard I was working in school and in my workbook. He said that being at level 3 in my fourth week was very rare for students.

But now we were in the fifth week of my stay. When I came home from school on that Monday, I looked on the board. It said three things: "Greg Vogt. Weekly chore is mopping floors. Level 4."

Before I could even process it in my mind, all my housemates in Timber were taking the words out of my mouth. "Greg! Dude, you're level 4!" they kept screaming. I was shocked. I was happy that I was at level 4 because I now had the privileges of going off campus one day per week, having porch time, single-handedly controlling the television on NFL Sundays, and I could even get an on-campus job if I wanted. But I was more shocked than happy. Shocked because the staff members and my therapist said I was the quickest person to reach level 4 coming into Key Ridge since they could ever remember. Maybe the quickest person ever to reach that goal in the school's history.

Since that day, my mind-set gradually began to change. Or should I say I gradually began to change my mind-set. I began to grow the smallest bit of hope again back in my life. Having the combination of making a great catch in the championship game and knowing that I was one of the only people to reach level 4 in a short amount of time due to my hard work seemed too good to be true. Some people never reached level 4 in one full year at Key Ridge. I was able to do it in five weeks. A lot of credit went to Brett for trusting me that I was working hard to improve myself and confirming that I deserved to reach level 4. But ever since that day, I felt more alive inside and had some hope shine into my struggling mind each and every day. When I had very down days, it was still brutally hard to deal with. But I just tried to think of what I had recently accomplished to push me forward. The fact that I put myself in the position to succeed in the workbook, and make the catch in the football game, was a huge step in the right direction. Because before that, I did essentially nothing to develop myself. Even though it was just one catch and moving up to a certain level, these two things were enough to bring some life back into my aching mind.

10

Big Shot on the First Visit

November had rolled around, and it was approaching my seventeenth birthday. This meant that no matter how bad I could have screwed up in my time at the school, I would be discharged once I turned eighteen because Key Ridge sent you out into the real world when you're eighteen. The facility wasn't allowed to keep anyone above that age no matter how bad off that person may be. You either had to graduate or you just became discharged before your eighteenth birthday. Or I guess if you were really in the dumps, you'd get sent off to a treatment center for adults.

So my seventeenth birthday was nothing special, as expected. I don't even remember what I did on my birthday at Key Ridge. It was an ordinary day. I think I was allowed to call my parents on that day for a quick talk, but even that was a blur. All the boys in my cabin would ask me what I was doing for Thanksgiving. I didn't really know what they meant because I was just planning on doing whatever we as a cabin would do that day. But the reason they asked was because if your therapist had enough confidence in you to let you have a visit, then you could be discharged for a week or so to go home for the holidays. Unfortunately, Brett was still a bit hesitant, despite my progress. Although he admitted and praised me on how well I was doing, he still was afraid. He knew that just only about a month ago I had tried to take my own life. He thought it was much too quick to be able to allow me to go off campus. I had a track record of depression and irrational decisions stemming from that. So he admitted to me that he was scared and nervous to let me go out of the secluded property of Key Ridge. I asked him if I could have a visit like the rest of my friends, and he simply said no.

So Thanksgiving is usually a happy, joyful time with family as you're feasting together with big smiles and endless hugs to go around. But for me, I was stuck on campus with no family. Out of the fifteen boys in Timber, four of us remained on campus over Thanksgiving. Everyone else was on a family visit. It was lonely and quiet. I just wanted to see my family. I wanted to give them hugs and apologize. I wanted to try to convince my little brother that his big brother was doing a little bit better. I wanted my mom's delicious home-cooked Thanksgiving meal, where there was not a worry in the world besides a food coma. But there was nothing I could do about any of it. I ate the meal that the cafeteria made for us. It was turkey with gravy, mashed potatoes, spinach, and stuffing. It was mediocre, and I was now really craving my mom's home-cooked Thanksgiving dinner.

When the guys returned from their visits, I was very glad. It made me miss them more than I had imagined. It was good to see the energy back in the house full of fifteen people. I started being more active in various activities on campus the more I got settled in. We would have pool time once a week, which I thoroughly enjoyed, not only because it was a new form of fun exercise but also because our pool instructor was very nice and energetic. She had a hilarious personality.

I also began engaging in horse therapy. Each person had the option to attend horse therapy for one hour each week. Key Ridge had a horse stable filled with dozens of beautiful horses. At first, I was not too fond of this, but I decided to give it a shot. It was surprisingly really enjoyable and peaceful. It was a nice getaway from all the constant commotion of fifteen loud boys in one house. I learned how to take care of the horses and clean their hooves. I learned how to prepare the horse for riding and put on their harnesses and gear. Lastly, I got a lot of experience riding different horses. The horse trainers would give me my boots and my cowboy hat and just like that, I got to ride one new horse each week. When I liked a certain horse, I would request him or her for the following session. As I would get more experienced and build trust with certain horses, I would be allowed to trot. Eventually in the later stages, I was riding horses that would jump over hurtles and go across an obstacle course. I felt like a cowboy. I continued riding horses for my entire yearlong stay at Key Ridge. I found it very therapeutic and thrilling.

I decided to take part in the on-campus church every Sunday, too. That was interesting for two very different reasons. The first one being that I hadn't gone to church since I was a little kid, so it was a big change for me. The other reason that Sunday church was interesting was that this was one of the only times where it was allowed for girls and guys to be in the same room together on campus. I won't beat around the bush when I say this, but being able to see girls was a major reason I attended the one-hour church sessions each week. We weren't even allowed to sit next to them, talk to them, or even look at them, and vice versa. If a staff member saw somebody conversing or even looking extensively at the opposite sex, that person would be given a major warning and in some cases escorted out of the church. But still, no words can describe how difficult it was to live a daily lifestyle without interacting with girls. This drove me nuts, so that is part of the reason why I found church enjoyable to attend. Just to be around girls, to be in the same big room as them, felt good. Sadly, I found this to be the driving reason to attend church at that point in time, rather than honoring God. My priorities were not intact, and neither was my mindset.

In early December, we were given the word that basketball season was beginning. I was ecstatic, and so were Peyton and many other people around campus. Timber began practicing on a consistent basis. During our gym time every lunch and dinner, we would design plays and scrimmage against each other. Although I never reached my goal of playing on my high school varsity basketball team, I became a better basketball player at Key Ridge than I was at McKinney High School, and even than I had been on the Defenders during my travel ball days. I would practice every day, multiple times per day, because there was only so much you could do on a campus where you weren't allowed to leave or make your own choices. So I used basketball as a point of therapy and as a point of release. As a result, I became the best version of myself as a player. I loved how seriously Timber took sports and that Tom and Mike would lead the way with that intensity.

The season was twelve games long before playoffs would happen, and by the middle of December, we had reached a record of four and one. Our one loss, well, take a guess. Cabin 8. I personally thought Peyton was the best player in the school, and so did many others. He would average about twenty-five points, eight assists, and eight rebounds per game, all as the shortest player on the court. Some other people thought Reece for Cabin 8 was the best player. He was hard to guard in the post and could dunk with ease. He was lengthy and could even step out and shoot a good jump shot and three-pointers. Believe it or not, I was considered one of the better basketball players in the school myself. Those words sounded like a foreign language to me after what I went through in my two years of basketball at McKinney High. Out of just about 125 boys at Key Ridge, I was considered to be in the top five by most people. It motivated me because I wanted to help Peyton lead our team to a championship, especially after still having the sour taste of football season in our mouths. Peyton and I had great teamwork on the court, which made our team very good.

Our coach and lead staff member, Tom, took me aside to talk to me one day. He asked me if I knew about the all-star teams that we put together for Key Ridge. I didn't know what he was talking about. He explained to me that there were essentially two leagues for each sport Key Ridge took part in. There was the league that was restricted to Key Ridge only, where each cabin played each other. I knew about that one, of course. But then he explained the all-star league. For each sport, the head coaches selected who they wanted to be on the Key Ridge all-star team. The team was composed of the top twelve best players on campus who obtain over a 3.0 GPA. The all-star team went out and played other all-star teams of local organizations or treatment rehabilitation centers. I was selected to be on the all-star team, which I was very excited about. This meant that not only would I play to represent Timber in the on-campus school basketball league but also to represent Key Ridge as an entire school in the all-star league. Three Timber boys were selected to be on the team: Peyton, Lance, and myself. The remaining nine came from other units, and our starting center was Reece, as expected. Between December and February, basketball really became a huge part of my daily life. Not only would I play with friends at lunch and dinner breaks, but I would also have team practices a couple days each week for Timber and the Key Ridge all-star team. This was awesome because it meant less downtime in the house.

When I played my first game with the all-star team, it was a major wake-up call. The competition was similar to that of high school junior varsity and varsity players. But what I was used to playing against were most kids at Key Ridge who never played the sport competitively. The all-star team was different because it was the best players from our school playing the best players from another. By the middle of December, we posted a record of two and three. There were no playoffs or championship game in the all-star league, so the record wasn't as critical. It was more so just play a single game and try to win that game. And we would do that a couple dozen times throughout the season. We still worked our tails off to win every game we could. Similar to the on-campus league, there were twelve total games played in a season, usually once every Saturday.

It was a few weeks away from Christmas time, and I began wondering if Brett would allow me to go home for a visit. So in my therapy session, I asked him. "Brett, what do you say that I'll be able to go home to visit my family for Christmas?" I asked. He responded, "Well, Greg, I see where you would want that; however, I still think it is too soon for me to let you go home for a period of time."

I was frustrated, and I let him know it too. He then

said, "But I have the next-best option for you. Instead of you going to visit your family, I will allow your family to come out to Meridian to visit you, and you can stay with them off campus at their hotel. You would be given five full days with them to do whatever you want around the local Meridian area."

His point was that even though I would still be off campus, being close to the property would diminish the likelihood of me making an irrational decision, which was his fear. My parents didn't really know what to think, as they had not seen me for over two months since I waved good-bye to them in the parking lot. So they usually stuck with Brett's word and trusted him. I don't blame them, as he was a great person. But at the same time, my parents did also think it was best for me to be near Key Ridge, as much as they wanted me home. They did not know how I really was doing on the inside, even though I was telling them I was doing well and improving, which I was. But to them, they couldn't tell if I was hiding some inner feelings or not. So Brett and my parents wanted to be safe and have an "Idaho visit." I was content, and didn't argue the fact why I wasn't allowed to go home. I was just looking forward to seeing my family again, and not relying on the twenty-minute weekly phone calls to get by. My family came out to Meridian to visit me from December 21 to 26, some of the final days of 2010.

Their flight got in at 3:00 p.m. on the twenty-first, and they were set to pick me up from Timber around 4:00 p.m., as it was about an hour drive from the nearest airport. I had school that day, and it felt like the longest day ever. The hours felt like days, and the minutes felt like hours. But once the bell rang and I headed back to Timber, I grew even more eager and excited. I was kind of nervous and anxious though because I hadn't seen my family in over two months. I rarely would talk with them since I wasn't allowed. The last time I had seen them was when we had tears running down our faces in the middle of the parking lot of the mental hospital as they watched me leave with Mark. So this time around, I was anxious but excited. They pulled up to the front and walked up to our porch. I opened the front door and ran into my family's arms. The happiness I felt was amazing. And the joy they had was unbelievable. I had finally seen my family for the first time since being sent away to a different state to go to rehab. It felt surreal. It felt like six months of being away from them instead of two.

During those five days, we shared many special memories together. We went to many great restaurants to get me real food instead of treatment center food, went sledding down the snow slopes, and saw the nature of Idaho. But nothing compared to just being in each other's arms, talking, laughing, and smiling. This was the first time that they had seen me with a smile on my face in a long time. We had tons of things to catch up on. I mean, just think where we left off: waving bye to each other in the parking lot of a mental hospital as a giant guy escorted me away to another state to go to rehab. My parents asked me a lot of questions and were still just as concerned as ever about my well-being. All they wanted was for me to enjoy life without having to fight through my depression. I told them that I was doing better and was in a stable environment. I had made a wide range of new friends. I had built up a little more confidence by playing sports and reaching level 4 on my personal path to doing well at Key Ridge. I enjoyed the nature, the beauty of the campus, and the peacefulness of the horses. I enjoyed having the honor of playing basketball with such a good player, Peyton. I enjoyed all the wonderful staff members who were helping me improve my life. I told them all these things, but I also said how hard it was to wake up each day and force my mind and body to do the same exact routine every single day. I mentioned how brutal it was that we weren't allowed to see or interact with girls. I said how we didn't have much freedom and couldn't even go off campus or have a phone or a car. Nothing really.

I just had to make the most of what I had, which was fifteen guys in one house, a beautiful campus surrounded by nature, helpful staff members, fun sports, and the opportunity to either turn my life around or let the depression swallow me as a whole. Just the fact that I was able to say these things gave my parents more confidence in me. I was still depressed, even in December, and they knew that, and so did Brett. However, it was on a much less severe level. It wasn't quite life threatening anymore. My parents were very open with talking to me about anything, good or bad, and how I was feeling. But my little brother, Josh, who was thirteen at the time, really just wanted to have memorable times and fun experiences with his big brother before we had to part ways again for another couple months. We shared many laughs and good times. I was just doing my best to make sure that he didn't lose hope in me and that I could turn out to be a good big brother, despite not showing that in recent years. He still loved me, which was all I could have asked for. Josh means the world to me, as do my parents.

The day after they arrived, I had a basketball game with the Key Ridge all-star team. My family thought it was terrific how I was on the team and was trying to move past the damage that Coach Norris caused me in high school. They really wanted to come to my game to watch me play. It was weird to think that the last time they had watched me play was in the game of the incident with Coach Norris. But I was excited that they wanted to come watch me. This was coincidentally a home game for us, so we were playing right on campus at the Key Ridge gym. When the all-star team played at Key Ridge, the entire school would come watch, including girls, similar to the championship football game. But this was different because my family was also in the stands. There were a total of about one hundred people in the stands for that game, which felt like thousands to us. We were playing a really good team who was ranked second in the league. Before this game, my season high in a game out of the first five games for the all-star team was eight points. In the beginning of this game, I got off to a quick start and scored two baskets. The game was close through the first and second quarters.

It was the final play of the second quarter, and our team was inbounding the ball from the other team's side of the court. The other team was full-court pressing us, so we had to quickly get the ball in bounds. Peyton passed it in to me on the right side of the court, still eighty feet away from our basket. I took two dribbles to advance myself up the court as far as I could before the buzzer sounded. I launched a sixty-foot shot from the opposite three-point line. It was in the air for a couple of seconds. The faces of the audience were following the ball ever so closely. And there it was. Swoosh! The crowd erupted. I just drained a sixty-foot buzzer-beating three pointer to send our team into halftime with a two-point lead. To this day, that is the most ridiculous play I have ever done in any sporting event. My parents were there to witness it, and they were baffled, along with the rest of the crowd and even my teammates and coaches. Personally, I couldn't even believe it myself. The other team was shocked, and it was a big momentum changer. We went on to win that game 67–61, and I scored a season-high seventeen points in front of my family. They must have brought me some good luck because that was by far the best game I played that season. It was an incredible experience to play in front of them and especially to make that shot and beat one of the best teams in the league.

After the game, my family and I went back off campus, as we only had a day and a half left of being together. We spent quality time, and it was so nice to be with them again. Before they left for the airport, we hugged and kissed each other good-bye. I told them that I was thankful for having them in my life and supporting me. I told my brother that he was my best friend, because I was unsure if he still thought that, considering my recent selfish actions. It was hard to keep the tears from falling as my family was leaving. I had no idea when the next time I could see them again would be.

11

A New Year

When I went to school on that Monday after the visit with my parents, I saw posters in the hallways that I would have never expected. It was pictures of me making the sixty-foot shot in the game on Saturday. I knew that there was a cameraman during the game, but I had no idea that the school would post it all around for everyone to see. Similar to the football game, people were coming up to me congratulating me on the shot and saying how crazy it was. I'll admit, to make a shot from that far took some luck. I was trying to be humble about it, but it was cool to see the action photo shots around campus.

The Key Ridge all-star team went on to take third place in the league. I loved every second of it, as it was great being able to play more competitive basketball again. It gave me good memories of the days when I played travel club ball with the Defenders.

The championship game for the Key Ridge on-campus league was soon to be played, as it was the middle of January 2011. Take a guess as to which two teams made it to the finals. Yes, you are correct: Cabin 1 and Cabin 8. I called it the battle between Peyton and Reece, as that is really what it was all about. The majority of everyone else were role players, including myself, but those two guys dominated every sport they played, no matter who they were playing against. I was hyped. Our team was hyped.

The crowd was wild. It was loud in that gym, and I felt the energy. I was more excited for this than the football championship because I am more of a natural basketball player and felt more comfortable using my skills to help the team win. Both teams had the same record. In the entirety of the season, both squads had only lost once. Cabin 1 beat Cabin 8 one game. Conversely, they beat us in another game. It was as even a championship game as could be expected. It nearly mirrored how the football game was played. This game was so close from the very start to the bitter end. Eventually, with a couple of big defensive plays late in the fourth quarter, Timber would prevail! We beat Cabin 8, 62–56. Peyton dropped twenty-two points and nine assists. Reece had eighteen points and fourteen rebounds in the loss for Cabin 8. I ended up with eleven points and had some timely shots that helped secure our team the championship trophy. It was our first championship since I had been at the school, so it was an awesome feeling knowing that we were the most recent champions on campus. The feeling of revenge was so sweet for us, but so bitter to Reece and his unit. They were furious, as this rivalry was the fiercest on campus. Though we were all friends, every time Cabin 1 played Cabin 8 in sports, it was a dogfight.

After every sports season, Key Ridge held an end-of-the-season ceremony. It was a giant banquet where each team and their coaches would sit at a designated table. It was a great event, as everyone was catered a delicious meal and celebrated the season. The staff put together a big slide show for everyone to watch with the season's top plays. It was cool to see my big shot on the projector, but the best part was the last picture of Timber holding up our trophy together. I was always the happiest when other people found success and contributed in a team aspect, rather than focusing on individual achievements. Like they always say, there is no *I* in *team*. However, they awarded many honors and medals. Some included: best team, most improved player, best scorer, best rebounder, best defender, best assist leader, best team player, best coach, and also MVP. It was all a surprise to see who was awarded each honor, so everyone was very eager to hear the announcements at the end of the banquet.

Timber got best team, Tom got best coach, and Peyton got best assist leader, all representing our cabin with full pride. Best scorer and rebounder went to Reece, and the other remaining honors went to well-deserving players on other cabins. I thought that I might get awarded best team player, but once that was given to someone else, I was content not being awarded anything besides a team champion, which mattered the most. That is how I modeled my game, to do a little bit of everything well and to be an unselfish player to help our team win.

The commissioner saved the MVP award for last. "This player was dominant on both ends of the court. Quick as lightning and hustled every play. His shot was nearly perfect, and his ability to get to the basket was easy. He looked to get his teammates open shots but led his team to victory when needed."

Everyone looked at each other as the entire room started chanting, "Peyton! Peyton! Peyton! Peyton!"

Before the commissioner said the name of the MVP he had described, he announced, "For the first time in the history of basketball at Key Ridge, we are awarding a co-MVP this year!"

Everyone was shocked and excited to see who it would be. I thought it would be ridiculous for it to be anyone other than Peyton or Reece.

The commissioner carried on, "Though relatively new to the school, this player played his heart out each and every game. He helped his team by providing individual success while also giving his teammates many shining moments. He hit timely shots in close games and made for an unbelievable duo with Peyton. He is known to have hit the longest shot that we know of today from well beyond the half-court line. So with that being said, the co-MVP goes to both Peyton and Greg of Timber!"

I was at a loss for words. The room went wild and was cheering ever so passionately. Peyton hugged me and screamed in my face, "Let's go!" He was pumped, and so was I. As we both walked up to receive our individual trophies, I briefly approached Cabin 8's table and found Reece sitting there, clapping for me with a big smile on his face. I went up to him and whispered in his ear, "This should have gone to you. You deserve it." I meant that with all my heart. Peyton and Reece were by far the two most talented basketball players that Key Ridge had. I'm sure Reece would have gotten it if they had beaten us in the championship. But I gladly accepted the honor and celebrated with Peyton and the rest of Timber. All the guys said how proud they were of me, and our staff members were so excited for us. I couldn't believe it. I sometimes wonder that if I hadn't hit that long shot, or if we hadn't won the championship, if I would have still gotten the award or not. Probably not. But all was well because Peyton and I were co-MVPs of the school, and Timber had the championship. The championship was really all that mattered.

It really began sinking in that I had begun doing some good things with my life. I was helping my sports teams win, received individual honors, advanced up to level 4 in my program, and was still doing well in school.

Most important, my suicidal thoughts began to diminish month after month that I was at Key Ridge. Certainly visiting with my family was a huge help, but also the care of the staff members, the new friends I was making, and the new atmosphere of Key Ridge helped me thrive more than usual. I was no longer sulking in the corner with my hood on, thinking about what a terrible person I was like I did at McKinney High. I got away from the consistent depressed state of mind. I escaped the toxic environment and the bad situations I got myself into with Sofia and Coach Norris. I was in a new, comforting environment, away from home.

Though each day was hard at Key Ridge, I began to realize that this was becoming a good decision. I was still depressed, because depression does not leave overnight. In some cases it never leaves. So it was still a constant battle overcoming depression and seeing life on the bright side, even while at Key Ridge. But it was much less severe and was no longer life threatening. I was at least functional and able to put a smile on my face. That was a difficulty at McKinney High. Just smiling couldn't be done. That's how bad it was. And having breakdowns was a daily thing. Now it was different. With my hard work and new influences, I began making small changes to improve myself.

During therapy with Brett one week in the middle of January, he suggested I do something that made me very uneasy. He knew how miserable my experience was at McKinney High, so he suggested deleting every single person, one by one, off my social media outlets. He knew I never talked with them, and that they weren't really there for me. So his point was that unless they were great friends, why have them there? Although I hadn't been on social media or technological services for four months, he told me to sign in on his computer in his office and do this. He said the sooner you do it, the easier the transition will be of letting go and moving on. Once I went on social media again, seeing all those people would bring back bad memories. Also, some of them were just disrespectful to me, so there was no point in having them on. Some of the people who I deleted were easy. But it was my "closer friends" at McKinney High who were difficult. I thought they were close, but in reality they weren't. The reason why Brett and I even chose to delete those people was because he helped open my mind to realize that they were not actually true friends. I thought they were true friends in my immature state of mind. But all they really did was crack jokes about me and weren't supportive when I needed it most. So boom. One by one I deleted hundreds of old acquaintances from my Facebook. Literally deleted hundreds on that day.

And there it popped up — the name. The most difficult person for me to see: Sofia. Brett knew everything about her from what I had told him, and he said, "Just go ahead and click delete." I was so hesitant, as this girl meant so much to me at the time. I began having major flashbacks and was staring at the screen in disbelief. Unfortunately, my desire for her was a big part of why my life went downhill so quickly. She hadn't reached out to me in months, even to see how I was doing. Almost nobody did, which was why Brett suggested deleting each of them. Most people knew me as "the kid who tried to jump off a balcony, aka Greasy Greg." Not many people took it seriously, and I felt that very few people cared. And that's okay, because I soon realized who my true friends were. It was not those people, and it was not many.

I realized that I had two real, true friends at that point in time. Yes, two. It was difficult to admit to that, being a seventeen-year-old boy. Most people at that age want a plethora of friends. The first of my two friends was Isaac. From the day we met on the basketball court in sixth grade and still to this day, we remain close friends. He was one of the rare ones that actually stuck with me during my low McKinney points. The second true friend of mind was a girl by the name of Ashley. Ashley and I met in 2009 on a cruise to Alaska. She went with her family, and I went with my family. On the ship, they had a teen's club, where we met. I was fifteen and she was thirteen at the time. We would go on to have a terrific week on that cruise and grew close within just one week. She lives in Canada, but to this day, we still remain good friends. Along with my family, Ashley was the one person who I consistently wrote letters back and forth to while in Idaho. I would wait a few weeks in between to receive her next letter, but it always made my day when I saw that I had mail from her. She had always been very supportive and is one of the kindest people I have ever had the pleasure of knowing.

But as I sat and looked at Brett's computer screen, I realized how hard it was to actually delete Sofia. Even thought it was just social media, I knew that this meant that I would be no longer interacting with her in real life either. It would be the final separation point, the good-bye point. But I did it. I clicked the button. Sofia was gone from all my social media accounts, and I essentially had no contact with her or anyone else back at McKinney High, except for a couple people who showed they cared by respectfully reaching out. It was hard, and Brett knew it was hard for me. I kind of thought he was crazy for suggesting to do this, but a couple weeks later, with counseling and lots of personal reflection, everything began to fall into perspective even more.

12

Me Against Myself

When the kids would occasionally tell me, "You messed up by trying to kill yourself. That's stupid. You're better than that," it was hard to take in. I thought it was disrespectful and not something that I wanted to hear. It frustrated me. I was already ashamed of what I did, so I hated talking about my depression and suicidal thoughts. It made me self-conscious and made me feel weaker than everyone around me. These were the kids that never faced depression and were the ones more into the drugs and gangs. But when I met people who had depression, they sympathized with me more. Everyone has a different opinion on this sort of subject. But hearing the harsh criticism made me tougher inside. I was a very immature kid, so spending time at Key Ridge grew me up a bit, mainly because of the people I was surrounded by and being away from home.

Although only a handful of people would say those harsh words to me, I really thought about it and analyzed what made them say that. But when I pondered about these points, I began to see both sides of the equation.

The first side: This is the side that I had only thought about while submerged in everything I was going through. The basis of my thought process was, "I don't want to deal with life's challenges anymore, so I am going to end it." In my mind, I saw that as the best decision at the time. The depression was grueling and painful to deal with day in and day out, each second of the day. Not many feelings are worse than going to the bathroom in the middle of class to cry. I hated myself and where my life was. I saw no point of continuing life, and I saw no good in it. My attitude was extremely pessimistic and irrational. I felt that everyone was out to get me, and questioned why I was going through hardships. I didn't even consider myself as the possibility of being the root problem. The thing that people didn't understand was that it was beyond difficult for me to control it. I felt that I had no control over my depression. Do you think I purposely tried to be depressed? Of course not. So dealing with something when you feel out of control is one of the most brutal obstacles one can face. The depression had full control over me. In my high school days, I didn't even know that what I was doing was selfish because I felt out of control. My mind was sheltered, and I didn't see the big picture. It didn't occur to me that if I did actually die, that it would affect other people, not just myself. I had blinders on. The depression was a monster.

I later came to realize that no matter how depressed I may have been, I still had the capability, willingness, and ability to make my own decisions, for the worse or for the better.

So here is the second side: Now that I had been erased from my previous high school environment, I had a more stable place to reflect. Hearing all the opinions and viewpoints at Key Ridge put things in perspective for me more. Therapy, working to personally grow myself, and conversing daily with people who also had problems in high school really helped me as an individual. I committed my mind and heart to making changes. And during my months at Key Ridge, my knowledge and understanding of my decision-making process began to improve. I now understood why people would say something like "You're stupid for trying to take your own life." It all started to hit me.

I was facing a battle against myself. In high school, it was a battle between trying to fit in with the high school crowd and with really doing what made me happy. I did nothing that made me happy. Nothing. Ever. I thought it was basketball, but it wasn't. I thought it was Sofia, but it wasn't. The only thing that could have made me happy was my perspective and my choices, which I never put to good use. I had resentment and anger as to why people at McKinney High didn't choose to reach out to me during my worst times. But now I know why. I was so unapproachable and closed off that nobody wanted to hang out with me. I don't blame them. Would you want to hang out with someone that walks around with a black hood covering his head and goes to the bathroom to have mental breakdowns each day? I sure wouldn't.

In my years at McKinney High, it was hard to realize, because I was that person. But now, it all made sense. It didn't really matter to most of them that I was depressed or suicidal. All they cared about was their own well-being, happiness, and personal growth as high school kids. I am referring to the high school population as a whole. I did receive personal affection from a few individuals, especially Ashley, Isaac, and my family, of course. But I realized that it all made sense. I remember Sofia always asking me if I needed anything or what she could do to help me. Before I went to Key Ridge, she was always trying to be helpful. She was one of very few who showed that. But I always turned her down. I said, "No, I'm fine."

I did whatever I could to make myself seem less vulnerable around her and to make it seem like I was doing okay. But by doing that, I turned her away and misinterpreted that she didn't care, when in reality, she always cared. It was me who didn't allow her help. She was trying, and I blocked her out because I didn't want her to think of me in a lesser manner. I was unwilling to receive any help from people. To put it all in perspective, I was battling myself. Me against myself is what it was. I was my own worst enemy. It was all me causing my own problems. It wasn't anybody else. I was unwilling to receive help and tried to handle everything on my own. I failed miserably. I realized that nobody caused me more heartache, pain, and grief than myself.

Even though I didn't have ideal circumstances with the basketball coach, there was a girl who I couldn't get, and self-confidence was nonexistent, I still could have done things differently. I could have found another sport instead of creating more frustration in seeing Coach Norris each day. I could have faced the reality that Sofia would be with Jeff, and I could have moved on and created other opportunities for myself. I could have tried meeting other girls. I could have found other hobbies, activities, and friends to improve my self-confidence and outlook on life. I did none of these. In fact, I did the opposite of these and decided to self-destruct. And that is why I blame myself for my decisions, and I take full responsibility. It was my fault for not doing something to tame my depression before it was too late. It was my fault for being stubborn and unwilling to experiment with other options and possibilities. People could have always been nicer and more supportive, but I was allowing other people to run my life.

I was not doing myself any favors. I was battling myself. The fact that I was even able to admit to this and see a whole new perspective was a big step in the right direction.

13

Bloody Faces

I was making some significant progress, even just realizing what I had done in the past. With time, I admitted my mistakes and matured as a person. In early February 2011, Brett granted me the opportunity to finally be able to take my first visit home. It was a five-day trip. Key Ridge sent an escort with me to take me to the airport and drop me off. I had all my belongings, and I was ecstatic to return home for the first time since October. It was the first time since the incident. My parents were excited but nervous. They even admitted their apprehension to me. They were concerned because our house was three minutes away from McKinney High, and they thought it might act as a trigger for me to do something irrational again. Brett was confident in how I was improving, but he also had some concern. I assured them not to worry. But they knew what I had done just months ago, so they were worried. It turned out to be a great visit. We spent a lot of quality time together, but it felt strange returning home for the first time in four months.

When I would exercise at home, I didn't have a gym membership, so I would go to the rival high school to run on the track and run the stairs. I would not go to McKinney High. I didn't even want to look at it. When I would drive by, it would create guilt and jealousy in me. I had a lot of resentment for that place due to what I experienced. But overall it was a great visit back home.

When I returned back to Key Ridge, I had forgotten about what the routine process was until the big Samoan guy told me to strip down. Like the first time, they were checking for drugs, weapons, tattoos, gang symbols, and other things. I didn't even know the first thing about any of those, but it was just a standard procedure that each Key Ridge student had to endure when they returned on campus from a visit.

When I got back to Timber, I went upstairs to drop off my luggage and unpack. Nobody was allowed upstairs usually, unless you were a level 4 or 5, so being a level 4 granted me that right. When I entered my room, I saw a name change on the board. I had gotten a new roommate. He was a guy by the name of Cameron. When I first met Cameron, I was kind of intimidated. He was a big kid, both tall and broad. He had braces, freckles, and a long ponytail, and still looked like a badass. He was not only big, but he was also very angry to be at Key Ridge. He was not at all excited to be there, which was his new home for who knew how long. It could turn out to be a couple years because he was only sixteen. As Cameron settled in a bit and got used to the lifestyle change, he became nicer and easier to talk to. In fact, Cameron quickly became one of my closest friends. He turned out to be a funny, jolly guy as I got to know him. He was good at basketball and most other sports too, which made Timber even better. Having the combination of Peyton, Lance, Cameron, and myself play for Timber made other units fear us in sports. Peyton and Lance were already two close friends of mine, and we hung out frequently each day. Lance was one of my other roommates, so Cameron, Lance, and myself grew close. We got along well and always talked about what we wanted our lives to be like once we got to leave Key Ridge permanently. Even though Cameron was new to Key Ridge, he could only think about life outside it. Although the four of us were all very close, I saw that Cameron and Lance were better friends than anyone else. Those two grew close very quickly.

Lance had already been at Key Ridge for over a year and a half, so he was very much ready to leave. He had no indication that he was leaving soon though. Lance started to grow irritable over time. Not just because of being at Key Ridge for so long, but also because he grew in love with this girl named Monica that he met back at home on one of his visits. Based off the pictures I was shown, she was a pretty girl with long, bleach-blond hair. He would talk to me about ten times a day, saying how much he missed her and how he wanted to be with her forever. It was intense. I know I had made an irrational decision partially over a girl, but I learned from that. I knew not to do it again and to not let other people be in control of my life. So I was trying to give him suggestions on how to maintain his composure. I tried to advise him to play it cool and go with the flow. Lance was also a very competitive person and never liked being shown up or proven wrong.

A couple months later, soccer season started at Key Ridge. Cameron was not a good soccer player, so he would spend all his gym time playing basketball. Lance, Peyton, and I usually played with him, along with a group of other people, when we weren't practicing for soccer.

One day we were playing a pickup game of basketball in the gym after dinner, five on five. The game was competitive and began to get a little hostile. We mixed up the teams to make it fair. I was guarding Peyton, and Cameron was guarding Lance. We noticed that throughout the game Cameron and Lance were playing very physical, considering it was just a pickup game. They're both big, strong guys, which made things interesting. I will never forget what happened on the play that turned out to be the last one of that game.

It was a half-court set. My team was on defense, and Cameron was one of the players on my team. Lance and Peyton were on the other team. Lance's team had the ball, and the game was tied. He drove in hard to the basket. When Lance drove to the right side of the hoop, he aggressively nudged Cameron with his shoulder and attempted a layup. But Cameron knocked down Lance, which was a hard defensive foul. The shot didn't go in, and the foul didn't look to be intentional. It just looked to be a very hard foul. Everyone expected to resume play and that everything would be fine because Cameron and Lance were best friends. But the unexpected happened. Out of nowhere, Lance jumped up from the ground and quickly approached Cameron. Lance was inches away from Cameron's face. He was cursing him up a storm. Cameron was cursing back. Their foreheads were touching.

Before anyone could intervene, Lance threw the nastiest punch I have ever witnessed in person, right to Cameron's nose. Cameron stumbled down to the floor with blood oozing down his face. He got up after a few seconds and charged at Lance, punching him in the face. He didn't make full contact, so Lance grabbed him and threw Cameron to the ground again. Seconds later, Lance was repeatedly smashing Cameron's head into the hardwood floor. He got about four smashes in before a six-foot-four, 260-pound staff member charged over in three seconds and pounced on both of them, breaking up the fight. For about thirty seconds, I couldn't see their faces because the large, interfering man blocked my view. But when he got up, it was a nightmare. Both Cameron and Lance's faces were smothered with blood, and broken skin peeling down. Lance lost a couple teeth, which led me to believe that Cameron got a couple punches in while wrestling on the ground.

They were detained by security and brought to different exits of the gym. On their way apart, they kept cursing at each other at the top of their lungs. I hadn't seen that much hostility expressed between two people ever before. I sat in the corner of the gym by myself, trying to process what I actually just witnessed. I was stunned. My two close friends just tried to beat each other's heads off, essentially. What was more confusing is that they were so close with each other up until this incident. I was upset and wished I had been able to break it up, but they were so big that I would have done no good. None of the kids intervened because we stood no chance. My first thought was: Will the three of us ever be best friends again? My second thought was: They better learn to like ICU because they will both be in ICU for quite a while.

So there they went. The two of them were stuck in ICU for over a week. That was a living hell, I'm sure. Days in ICU consisted of staring at white walls with no windows because it was underground.

Eight days later, Cameron returned back to Timber. I was happy to see him and gave him a hug. He had stitches across his left eye and his nose. They both were known to have anger issues, so I asked Cameron if he was calmer after the eight days. He said yes. However, he was still furious at Lance for turning on him like he did. He said he never wanted to see Lance again and wanted him off Timber, if it were up to him.

But that week there was word on campus about

Lance's status. People were saying that Lance was leaving Key Ridge. "He's getting sent away. He's leaving Key Ridge for good. He's going to Arkansas." Not only was this incident severe enough to get Lance kicked out of Key Ridge, but it also could have landed him in what was said to be one of the most intense rehab centers in America, which was located in Arkansas. Cameron also mentioned that Lance's therapist wasn't all that impressed with his progress and that Lance's family back in Washington was still concerned about him. The basketball incident sent it over the top.

To this day, I still do not know if Lance actually ended up in Arkansas. That was just the rumor around campus. It sounded possible, but I never actually received confirmation on a yes or no from anybody. The staff members kept it hush-hush. None of the kids had contact with him due to not having access to phones. The staff members would not tell us what the status was on Lance. That led me to believe that he very well could have ended up at a more intense facility, but who knows. They just told us to let it go and move on. This was an unfortunate event to me because both Cameron and Lance were good friends of mine at the time. And to this day, I have not spoken to or seen Lance since the bloodbath that happened on the basketball court that dark evening.

14

Spring Things

Between March and June of that year, I experienced some new changes. Brett and my family finally began to fully trust me and who I was striving to become as a person. They knew I was still fighting depression regularly at Key Ridge, but they also knew that I had grown into a better version of myself than I was back home. They knew I was no longer suicidal. Yeah, I still had days where I would be depressed, but the thoughts of suicide had diminished. This gave them confidence in me. So as a result, Brett allowed me to have more visits. Just that spring season alone, I got to go home on two separate visits within a span of just a couple months of each other.

Back on campus, I experienced some changes and fun things that were going on. Our staff members in Timber created a March Madness unit-wide bracket. All fifteen of us competed and filled out a bracket as to which team we thought would win the NCAA Men's Basketball March Madness tournament. This was my first time ever doing it. I selected UConn as my winner, and I was the only kid who chose them. A few weeks later, guess which team ended up winning the championship? You got it, UConn. My prize was ever so glamorous: a free Slurpee from 7-Eleven.

On my visit with my parents, we talked about taking the SAT and ACT in preparation for college applications.

My dad wanted me to take both. My mom wanted me to take none. My dad thought I was capable of going to a university, while my mom sincerely thought I was not ready and should either stay at home or go to a community college at best.

One day my academic advisor, Harold, scheduled a phone appointment with my parents. Harold and I sat in a room discussing my future with my parents over the phone. My father said that he thought I had a future at a university when it was time to leave Key Ridge. My mom told Harold she disagreed. I remained quiet, as I really didn't know what to think. I was still rather insecure with myself, and my abilities, despite making some improvements in my life. My father suggested that I begin SAT and ACT preparation with Harold twice a week. Harold said he would be glad to do that. But Harold also told my father that he didn't believe I was ready for a university. He thought I was not set up for success and that I wasn't emotionally stable enough as an individual. The funny thing about this is that my father didn't really get too frustrated by Harold's claim. Everyone said what Harold was saying. My therapist, the staff members, my mom, friends, and others all thought that I didn't have what it took to be able to succeed at a university and survive in the new lifestyle.

So my Dad was used to hearing this from people. But this frustrated me and got me down. It made me feel stupid and that I had a bleak future ahead of me. It made me regret my past decisions even more.

Although Harold thought my parents should be concerned about sending me off to college right after Key Ridge, he told my father that he would willingly work with me on preparation for the SAT and ACT. My mother was upset at my father because she didn't want me taking these exams at all. She thought it would cause stress on me and that I wasn't emotionally stable enough to endure it. She had a fair point.

I decided to make a rather large change to my daily life at Key Ridge in March. The school put on a play once in the winter and once in the spring. Kids at Key Ridge volunteered their time to be a part of the school play and practice for a couple of months before the performance. The Meridian community came out to watch the performances once the play was performed. All the kids received the notice that we had the opportunity to be a part of the next school play, *Snow White and the Seven Dwarfs*. With no hesitation, I signed up. Not because I wanted to enhance my theatrical arts skills but because this was the only opportunity where we were allowed to fully interact with girls on campus. Sometimes we would go nearly a couple months without saying one word to a person of the opposite sex. So the thought of interacting with girls on a daily basis during play practice made me want to commit. Every evening all the crewmembers in the play would gather in the auditorium from 6:00 to 8:00 for play practice. Everyone in the play became friends very quickly, and it was always an uplifting environment. I had never envisioned myself being a part of a play production, but there I was. I had a relatively significant role in the play, as I was one of the dwarfs, Sneezy.

So each day on campus, the lifestyle grew a little more diverse. With studying for the big exams and play practice each day, my time was more occupied at Key Ridge than it had ever been. I still went to school each day, did therapy, played basketball, rode horses, swam, and engaged in soccer season for the school.

But since it was now spring and there were no more intense weather conditions, this made for the opportunity to do more outdoor activities. The recreation department of the school would go on endeavors every now and then off campus. You had to be a level 3 or higher to go, which fell in my favor. So that spring, I did a lot of things that I had never thought I'd ever do. While the snow was still fresh on the ground, we went snowshoeing one day. That was quite an experience. They even took us to the local amusement park. Another day, we woke up at 5:00 a.m. to hike a local mountain in Meridian. I had a backpack of water and some snacks. I also had a headlamp, so I felt extra cool. About twenty-five of us did this hike. It took us twelve hours to complete the seventeen-mile round trip hike. It was very difficult, but I had such a rewarding feeling afterward. The view was breathtaking, and the experience was one that I will never forget. Once we got down to the end, there was a small icy pond, probably one degree above freezing. We all jumped in to celebrate and then desperately got out within three seconds. It was the coldest feeling I had ever felt.

Another weekend, we actually took a two-night camping trip to the Sawtooth National Forest. Yes, you read that correctly. I got to leave campus for two nights, without it even being a visit with my family. We went with many staff members and all kids who were a level 3 or higher. Sawtooth is a beautiful place with great scenery. On that trip, I got to know a couple other people who I wasn't already particularly that close with. One was Jackson, who was Reece's secret weapon in sports for Cabin 8. He was good friends with Peyton. Another person who I grew closer with was a guy by the name of Mitchell. He was in Cabin 4. We would play basketball and football occasionally but didn't have much interaction besides that. Both he and I made every all-star team for Key Ridge sports, so we interacted through that. Other than that, we had never hung out much. On this trip, we hung out more, and I learned that he was a really good person with a funny personality. The second day that we were in Sawtooth, we all went white-water rafting. That is one of my favorite things to do, as I had previously been rafting in Yellowstone, Canada, and Northern California with my family when I was younger. It was a blast river rafting with all my friends and fun staff members. This was a spectacular trip, and it was nice to get away from the campus for a while.

A couple of months of studying went by, and it was finally the day to take my SAT exam. Harold set up an appointment for me to go to a facility off campus that was for test taking. It was a Saturday morning, and my appointment was scheduled for 8:00 a.m. I had a school soccer game at 12:30 that I didn't want to miss. I woke up bright and early, and the campus escort came and picked me up from Timber. I was nervous and anxious. Harold told me that I was the only kid at Key Ridge who elected to take the SAT so far that year. Most kids at Key Ridge either never took it, or they did it once they returned to their public high school back home. I felt a lot of pressure because I knew that nobody except my father believed that I was capable of going to college. Harold wanted to believe that I was, but he just had a cautious approach. He was so nice, and he didn't want to see me fail or be upset ever. So I think he was just scared to recommend to my parents to send me to college one day.

So here I was, taking this four-hour test that could define my fate with future college acceptances if it came to that. I got through the exam and was relieved when it was finished. My parents and Harold didn't set too high of expectations for me, given the circumstances I was in. Believe me, most Key Ridge students had tons to think about, but the SAT and ACT were not on the minds of many. I was still fighting a daily battle with depression, so it was a difficult task to study for these two tests for months and then to finally take them. The ACT was a week later, which I finished as well. I got my results back later on, and as expected, they were not scores to be bragged about. Both scores were below the average. Luckily, throughout my career at McKinney High and Key Ridge, I managed to earn a 3.5 GPA, despite dealing with many personal problems. My parents, Harold, and Brett were proud of me for even just taking the two daunting exams. Most kids on campus never took them, so they thought it was courageous of me to do that.

A couple weeks later, Timber won the school soccer championship. We were turning the sports tradition and making it our legacy. Back-to-back championships in two different sports at the school hadn't been done in years. It would have been three in a row if we had won the nail-biter in football.

By the end of June, it was finally time for *Snow White and the Seven Dwarfs* to take the stage. The school's auditorium seated over five hundred people. My family flew out from California just to watch me in the school play. I was embarrassed, but I had a very fun experience learning what it was like to be in a play and interact with many different roles and personalities. The costume changes were always fun. We had our last rehearsal hours before the first show. We performed the show three different evenings so that everyone in the local community had a chance of making it out to see the play one of the nights. There was a lot of hype and genuine excitement from the community of Meridian, so people were excited to see us perform. I was ready to show the crowd the best possible Sneezy that I could be. As we took our first set, we were all so excited but very nervous. Two and a half months of daily hard work was now finally being put together for three nights of shows. I knew my parents and Josh were in the audience, which made me ecstatic. All the teachers, staff members, coaches, therapists, and even the principal came to watch the performance. It turned out to be terrific and exceeded each one of our expectations. The crowd roared for us during intermissions and at the conclusion. Taking that final bow made me proud. I met up with my family after, and they were so happy and joyful to see what I had accomplished in being in the play. My dad chuckled and said that I must have been nervous on stage because "we could hear how heavy you were breathing through the microphone when you had a speaking part."

All three productions were fantastic, and completing the play was one of my most proud moments at Key Ridge. I felt like I accomplished something that I never even had a passion for. I never imagined myself being in a play at any point in my life, so it was special to be able to conquer something unique that took months to prepare for. It was also very nice to be able to talk to girls again for those months, but I was not looking forward to going back to the old ways of not being able to. Our daily practice sessions were the highlight of my day because of that. The play was professionally videotaped, and a video was given to each character in the play. The rest of that visit with my family was great, as was every visit with them. They repeatedly told me how proud they were of me and how far I had come at Key Ridge compared to where I was at McKinney High.

The summer months at Key Ridge didn't feel like summer months. The only significant difference was the warm, bright weather. But we still went to school each day and had our normal daily routine of getting up early and going to bed early. Oh yeah, and chores, lots of chores. My last home visit was scheduled for the first week of August. I was set to graduate that October. Baseball season was between the months of July and September at Key Ridge. This would turn out to be the last sport I would ever play at Key Ridge. I was fortunate to have been on every all-star team representing the school for all four sports. I met some great friends that way and created a competitive, fun lifestyle for myself. I was also fortunate in the fact that Timber made it to every single championship game in all four sports while I was there. We lost in football, but won in basketball and soccer. Now it was time for baseball. We made it to the championship, and unfortunately lost a close game, 7–5, against Cabin 4, which was Mitchell's team. For once, it wasn't Cabin 8. In a couple months, football would start up again, but I was set to graduate in the middle of the season, much before playoffs would even begin. Football was the one sport I never played a complete full season in at Key Ridge.

15

Escape to Down Under

During my last visit home, I finished up the process on getting my driver's license. I was almost done and set to take my test before I got to Key Ridge last October. Finally, I was able to accomplish that goal and obtain my driver's license. I was excited because I knew that in just a few months I would be back home, graduated from Key Ridge, and able to drive a car freely.

It was mid-August, which meant I had two months left at Key Ridge. I had already been at rehab for ten full months. I was ready to leave. The play was a couple months prior, so I was starting to get irritable and annoyed that we weren't allowed to talk to girls again. More and more of my closer friends that I had made were getting discharged, which meant they would never return to Key Ridge again. They would go back home to finish high school, or they would graduate and leave Key Ridge. A couple of kids graduated on campus, but not that many compared to how many people were just discharged from the program due to turning eighteen. The combination of my friends leaving, not being allowed to talk with girls, and that I had been there for ten full months already began to chip away at me. As great and helpful as Key Ridge was, I was growing frustrated and just desired to live a life outside of a treatment facility. I wanted more freedom with no restrictions. I wanted to be able to make my own decisions and live my life how I wanted to. I tried keeping the end goal in mind, that it was just two more months away and then I was free to go. But it was hard to keep that balanced mind-set.

One day, my threshold broke. I couldn't take it anymore. I felt so irritable, and I wanted to just go home. I needed a change. I was sitting on the couch in our living room, and I asked Tom if I could go outside for some porch time to catch some fresh air. Since I was a level 4, he said yes. I stepped outside and stayed there for a few minutes. Nobody else was on his or her porches from other units, so I took off running. For whatever reason, I thought it was a good idea to go AWOL and try to leave campus for a while. About two minutes of running later, I was tracked down and tackled by security. I was escorted back to campus, which wasn't a long way, considering I didn't get very far.

Then it hit me as to where I was going. It certainly wasn't Timber. It was ICU. All the staff members in there were shocked when they saw me. Everyone on campus knew me as a very well-behaved kid. I stayed at ICU for two nights, which was as miserable as it sounds. White walls, no fresh air, no windows, and some occasional meals are what it consisted of. I talked with one of the staff members who worked in another cabin and that I had grown pretty close with over the ten months. He said I was crazy for doing this. Not because I was actually crazy but because I was just about sixty days from leaving for good. He told me to put it all in perspective and keep my act together, and just push through it one day at a time for the next two months, but it was just too much for me to bear. I enjoyed Key Ridge and appreciated what it did for me. But I despised the feeling of being restricted.

Soon enough, I realized how stupid and irrational my decision was to run away from campus. It did nobody any good. In fact, later that week, Brett informed me that I would be dropped a level down to level 3 from level 4. I was upset at myself, mainly because I knew that I had been very close to reaching level 5 if I hadn't made any mistakes or bad decisions. But I faced the consequences for my stupid impulse decision. It didn't take me long to realize how foolish that was of me. I learned from it, and I was able to better keep my composure from then on.

When I returned to Timber from ICU, all the guys in the house came up to me asking why I did that. I told them it was because I wanted to leave and just couldn't take the feeling of being secluded anymore. They understood, but they were also very confused that it was me, of all people, to do this. AWOLs were somewhat common at Key Ridge, but more so for people who weren't leaving in the near future. My friends in Timber saw me as a leader in the house with a positive attitude and as a balanced thinker. That is who I turned out to be in my stay at Key Ridge, but I allowed my emotions to get the best of me during this incident. During this time, I was still battling depression and rather low self-esteem, though much improved from what it used to be. But these feelings did not play a major role in why I chose to run away. It was simply due to the build up of irritability and wanting a change. It was a stupid decision, a silly one really, because I wasn't even upset. I just felt trapped, and physically wanted something more.

Surprisingly, Brett and my parents weren't that upset or concerned with me. They both had extensive talks with me and made sure that I was emotionally stable afterward, which I was. I didn't choose to run away because I was suicidal or anything of that matter, and they understood the reasoning. They weren't concerned because they sincerely understood and imagined how hard it is to be at Key Ridge for one full year. It is grueling and frustrating at points. The feeling of not being in full power of your own daily life decisions took its toll on me after a while. So they sympathized and just made sure that I kept the grand goal in mind of graduating in mid-October. My other goal was to get back up to level 4 because I now knew that level 5 was out of reach.

16

A Swollen Graduation

After a slow-moving couple of months, the time was finally near. My graduation date was set for October 14, 2011. You might be thinking to yourself, October? Well, at Key Ridge, your graduating class was one person. Yes, one person. Every person had a different treatment plan and discharge or graduation date. Some would take a year, like myself. But I knew a couple people that were at Key Ridge for four full years, a young fourteen-year-old who grew up to be a graduated eighteen-year-old. Whoever was fortunate enough to graduate at Key Ridge had a graduating class of one: him or herself. I was so excited yet very nervous. I was eager to feel like I would be free again but also concerned to reenter the real world. I knew I was way behind everyone else back home in regards to doing normal high school things like meeting girls, applying for colleges, and hanging out with high school friends. So I was anxious to go home with a fresh start.

Four days before my graduation day, Timber went to the field to play a pickup game of flag football against each other for some fun. This would turn out to be my last time playing football with these guys ever. We played a scrimmage game for almost two hours and had a blast, until ...

My team was on defense, and Peyton was on the other team. On this one play, he played running back and went out for a screen pass on the left side of the field. I was the safety on that side and had the daunting task of trying to grab this speed demon's flags. He surged down the sideline as fast as lightning. I came across the field running as fast as I could to grab his flags and get him down. I reached him at the sideline and dove for his flags, as that was the only way he wouldn't get by me. Before I knew it, everything went dark. Boom.

I dove headfirst into the corner of metal bleachers. It was about three feet outside of the sideline and my momentum carried me face first into the sharp structured corner of the stands. Once I hit it, I bounced back like a rag doll and unleashed a terrifying scream of pain. I laid facedown in the grass, and my closed eyes saw stars. I heard everyone come huddle around me and ask if I was okay in a concerned tone of voice. I lay there motionless for nearly a minute before slowly raising my head a few inches off the grass. Once I did, everyone was grossed out. My face was sitting in a puddle of my own blood. My face looked like I just put it in a blender. It was scraped, puffy, and bleeding profusely. Still in excruciating pain, the first words that came out of my mouth were, "Damn, now I have to give my graduation speech looking like this on stage." The next sentence that I said was, "Did I get Peyton's flags at least?" Everyone had a good laugh. Surprisingly, the answer was yes. I am reluctant to say if it was worth it, but still, at least I got the flags.

Our staff lead, Tom, called security and rushed a golf cart out to the field to escort me to the health center. I called my parents explaining what happened, as I was in deep pain. They were upset to hear the news but thankful it wasn't worse. I was taken to the hospital, where they classified it as being a broken nose. I expected a concussion as well, but somehow I didn't end up with a concussion. So I got eight stitches, and there I was with a big patch on my face and a black-and-blue puffy nose.

The final couple of days passed, and I woke up on the morning of October 14, 2011, feeling like it was a dream. My parents and brother flew in the evening before, and I stayed with them in their hotel off campus. We arrived at 9:00 a.m. for my graduation ceremony at 10:00. It felt surreal, and it was hard to process what was actually happening. After being a Key Ridge student for exactly 349 days, it felt like that was my whole life. It felt so strange that it was all about to dramatically change. A couple weeks prior to the graduation, I created an invitation list of who I wanted to be in attendance at my personal ceremony. I invited every single guy in Timber and the good friends and staff members that I grew close with around campus. The graduation took place inside the church on campus. When I entered the building that morning with my mom, dad, brother, and Brett, the sight was breathtaking. We walked into a completely full room with not one seat empty. I was overwhelmed with joy and gratitude. It wasn't mandatory for all these people to attend, but they chose to anyway, for me. The principal told my family that this was the largest graduation ceremony he had ever seen for any student in his tenure at Key Ridge.

It was a very emotional ceremony. Many different people gave personal speeches, including Brett, Harold, Peyton, Cameron, a couple girls from the play, and a few of the staff members that I was really close to. Brett was trying to hold back the tears as he expressed how proud he was of me. He praised me for being a great kid and a hard worker and a pleasure to be around. Harold went up there with his charming smile and wonderful demeanor and told the audience of my successes in school, getting over a 3.5 GPA the whole year, and taking the two big exams. He explained how I was planning on looking into universities in the near future. Tom and Nolan, the two primary staff leaders in Timber, said how funny and positive I was on the unit. They gave funny examples about how I would scream at the television during a close sports game. Peyton and Jackson were naturally gifted musicians, so they performed a duet in my honor. Peyton played the saxophone while Jackson sang. My mother and father gave their individual speeches, which was really the first time that I felt like a proud son in a long time. I felt like I made them proud instead of making them worry about my old ways.

Then it was my turn to speak. I walked up to the podium ever so slowly. I looked at the audience and said, "Thank you all for being here. I am sorry you have to look at my face," referring to the football incident in a joking manner. I went on to talk for about five minutes, and halfway through came tears of both joy and sadness. I expressed how thankful I was to each and every person sitting in that room for helping me change my life and having a positive impact on me. I told them how I made great friends and many unforgettable memories there. I told them how my life went from near death to turning very positive and upward, largely due to the people who helped me improve daily. The tears of joy were because of how proud I was and dramatically happier I had become. The tears of sadness were genuine because I was upset about leaving my close friends and staff members, and I was scared to return to the real world. I was nervous to return to Simi Valley, where my bad history had taken place. The road ahead frightened me, and I was intimidated by words like *college* and *job*. That's why this day was so emotional. It was the end of my time at Key Ridge and the beginning of something new all at once.

Our recreational therapist put together a slideshow of all the great pictures and memories that were captured in my year at the school to be shown at the ceremony. I got to select two background songs to be played as the pictures were shown on the screen. I was given a select list, and I chose: "Good Riddance (Time of Your Life)" by Green Day, and "Wavin' Flag" by K'naan. Again, so many emotions of laughter, tears, inspiration, and joy were all brought about.

Following the ceremony, we had a gathering in the break room, where snacks and beverages were served. My family took countless pictures of all my friends, staff members, and me. The good-byes were the hardest part. There is a saying that goes, "It is not a good-bye but a see-you-later." But I knew in this case that most of them were real good-byes. And I was correct. Since my graduation day over five years ago, I have only seen a few Key Ridge people. So I wrapped up my good-byes, took a few last pictures with my family standing on the porch of Timber, and then we drove off. I looked back into the distance with tears dripping down my cheeks until I could no longer see Timber. That was it. It was all done. That was no longer my home. I was gone and off to a new chapter of my life. I was a Key Ridge graduate, in a graduating class of one person.

17

Returning Home

It felt surreal to step foot in my own home again, knowing that I would be living there for good now. There would be no more traveling back to Idaho. I was reunited with the three most important people in my life: my mom, my dad, and Josh. The transition back home was just very different. I had so much free time on my hands, with very few obligations. No work. No school. And I had very few friends from McKinney High. In fact, I hung out with zero people from McKinney High in the first couple of months back. I started to try to branch out a bit, by spending time with Isaac and his friends, who went to a rival high school. We always had a fun time when we were together.

As soon as I returned home, I started applying to colleges. My father helped guide me through the process. I ended up applying to seventeen different colleges. Because it was so rushed and there was lack of time, I didn't have the opportunity to research and explore different universities like most high school seniors were doing. I was already a high school graduate, while everyone else was still a senior in high school. Since I returned home in October, it made the college application process stressful. Due to a shortage of time and research, I applied to sixteen colleges in the state of California. My one out of state school: The University of Arizona. Between November and March, I was eagerly and patiently waiting for each school's letter in the mail.

The college application process was by far the biggest obligation I had at that point. The rest of the hours of each day were free. I often grew bored and lonely. It was becoming evident that I didn't have many friends after returning from Key Ridge. All my friends were essentially back in Idaho. One thing that I did was write letters to my friends still at Key Ridge, just like my family, Ashley, and Isaac did for me while I was there. I wrote to Peyton, Reece, and the Timber cabin as a whole. Every Friday evening, I would call Timber and they would put me on speaker and I would talk for about fifteen minutes with all of the guys. I told them how much I missed them, and they said the same toward me. It was hard transitioning from being with those people twenty-four seven, three sixty-five to not seeing them at all.

Just over one month after graduating, I was turning eighteen years old. I was excited, not just because it was my birthday, but more so because Ashley planned a visit to come see me in California for a week from Canada. Before that visit, I had not seen Ashley in over two years since we met on the Alaskan cruise. The time with Ashley was spectacular. We went to the beach, downtown LA, Hollywood, and other touristy spots around the area. I also introduced Ashley and Isaac to each other, which meant a lot to me, considering they were two of my close friends. It was a blast, and I was so grateful to have her out to visit me for my birthday. I told her how much her letters meant to me while at Key Ridge and that sometimes those were the only things keeping me going. She was one of my biggest supporters through my worst times, and I expressed to her how thankful I was for that.

In early December I got a call from one of the staff members at Key Ridge named Lenny. He was the sports commissioner in charge of running every sport and event that took place on campus. He also was in charge of the Key Ridge all-star teams and hosting every sports banquet following each season. He had a large commitment, and his passion was evident. We were talking for a while, and he was asking how everything was going for me. I told him all was well, and that I was just getting used to the whole change. Then he said, "Greg, I was thinking. You meant a lot to many people at Key Ridge through being a good friend and role model. You showed great success in your time here. How would you like to be the first person to do a live Skype session with entire school?" I was baffled, and muttered yes in excitement and honor.

One week later, the big Skype session took place. I went onto my computer at home and logged in. He gave me his username to be able to Skype him directly. Once we connected and the view of his screen came clear, I couldn't believe what I was looking at. It was the entire school — all the students and staff members in the big banquet room to hear me give a speech. My face was on the giant projector screen in front of them. I gave them the breakdown of how I was doing and what I was up to. The point of this was that Lenny knew that I was doing well and not getting into trouble. As difficult as this is to say, a lot of Key Ridge kids returned to old detrimental habits when they were discharged. He trusted me and knew that I had created a bright future for myself. So he asked me to mention to the kids what I was doing on a daily basis, how I was applying to colleges, spending quality family time, and thinking about my future. I also explained how I was able to thrive during my tenure at Key Ridge. I said that building relationships and cooperating with staff members were two key points. I mentioned that being active in wanting to improve in school, sports, hobbies, interests, and personal growth goes a long way. I reiterated how important it is to have a close connection with your family. I concluded by saying that if I was able to get through it, they would all be able to make it through too, as long as they worked hard and kept a positive attitude. Taking control of the situations that are controllable was another big point I told the kids.

It was a special experience for me to be able to give that speech to the entire school. It showed me that I was loved and appreciated by the people at Key Ridge. I felt very good and proud about that. I wanted the best for all the kids there, and I wanted to see each of them conquer their goals and live a healthy and happy lifestyle.

In late December my father came home from work one day with a large bag. He opened it up, and it was a scale. He said, "This is for you." He said that he thought I was gaining a little weight. The year prior, I entered Key Ridge weighing 155 pounds standing at five foot nine. In the middle of Key Ridge, I weighed in at 165 pounds and grew to be slightly over five ten. When I hopped on the scale, I was the same height but weighed in at 180 pounds. Keep in mind that this weight was essentially no muscle because I never worked out, aside from playing basketball. My dad just told me to monitor my weight and watch what I eat. The main reason for telling me this was that I had been on antidepressants for well over two years at that point and the depression medications seemed to be slowing my metabolism significantly and causing weight gain.

Despite the progress I had made on a personal level, I was still ordered by psychiatrists to be on medications. There was a long debate while I was still at Key Ridge between Brett, my family, my psychiatrist, and me. The debate was about which kind of depression I should be medically classified as having. My psychiatrist and my mother thought it was long-term permanent depression that would never go away. The psychiatrist told me to my face that I would have to be on medications for the rest of my life. I was furious and thought he was incorrect when he said that remark. My mom tended to agree with the doctor. But my dad, Brett, and I thought it was something else. Brett, my therapist, is a psychologist, of course, so he knows a thing or two about this subject. He explained how he thought I had situational depression, which meant that I would react to certain situations in a dramatic way, causing me the feeling of depression per each incident. Situational depression is controllable by the person though.

During all my worst incidents, I was taking the antidepressant medications. Due to this fact, Brett, my father, and I were a little skeptical that the medications were actually helping that much. But to the point of the psychiatrist, my depression turned out to be a multi-year ordeal that was a constant battle each day. But the difference was that I would only overreact in a negative way over certain situations, which didn't happen frequently. It only occurred over big things that meant a lot to me. So half the people thought it was permanent depression, while the other half, including myself, thought it was situational depression. Ultimately, it was up to me to "prove" to the doctors and my mom that I didn't have a long-term mental health illness and that it was just temporary and on a case-by-case basis. Either way, my depression would take control of me at times to the point where I was helpless. I still didn't know how to control it at times. So the psychiatrist ordered me to remain on the medications until he saw a stable track record of long periods of time with me not showing any symptoms of depression or suicidal thoughts. As a result, I saw an increase in weight gain, which raised concern from my father.

18

Heart-Wrenching

It was a brand-new year, the beginning of January 2012, and I was excited for what was ahead of me. I had already been accepted to a few colleges, including San Jose State University, California State University San Marcos, and California State University Dominguez Hills. I had rejections from several, such as UCLA, USC, and San Diego State University, to name a few. But I was glad to have been accepted to a few at this point. Although I didn't have much going on in my life and not many friends, being back home was going relatively well compared to the last time I was in Simi Valley.

One day I got a Facebook message from a person who I used to go to school with at McKinney High School. Her name was Emma, and she had graduated the year prior. We got to talking, and she asked me how I was doing and about my experience in Idaho. I told her I was doing better and briefly explained what living in Idaho for a year was like. A few days later, Emma messaged me saying that she wanted to meet up with me. I was a bit confused because I had probably talked to her only once in my life before this. But I didn't have much better to do, so I decided to meet up with her. She told me she would pick me up from my house. So on a Tuesday evening, I got in her car and we went off to the beach. We just had a casual walk and caught up on things. I barely even knew her, so it was definitely a different kind of situation. She said she was going to a local community college and working at a restaurant. She seemed like a nice girl, considering that was the longest I had ever hung out with her.

She then started asking about me. She knew about my incidents at McKinney High, and she asked why I chose to do what I did. I told her that I didn't want to live my life anymore because battling depression every day wasn't worth it to me. I told her that I thought lowly of myself and that I felt as if I didn't deserve good things in life. I mentioned that my poor relationships with Sofia and Coach Norris played a major role in my downfall and how I handled that adversity in an improper way. She asked all about Key Ridge and what the whole experience was like. I told her the main points, and I said how hard I worked to try to get my life back on track. I said I had changed it so much to the point where I hadn't felt suicidal in well over a year. Though still having depression and being on medications, I had made improvements in my life to have a more balanced approach on things. Emma was pleased to hear that I had gotten to the point where I was and that simply I was alive and well.

She knew I despised my high school experience, so later on in the walk she asked, "Contrary to the bad things that happened, what was your favorite part about going to McKinney High?" I responded by saying, "Nothing much really. But if I had to answer, I'd say a tie between my freshman year of basketball and hanging out with Ms. Reeves."

When I said that, her demeanor changed instantly. She got quiet. Emma looked at me with a blank stare and a weeping look in her eyes. She began trying to speak, but she was having trouble putting a sentence together. "What did you say?" she muttered.

She paused for about ten seconds, trying ever so desperately to put her thoughts into words. She asked me, "You didn't hear?" I shook my head in confusion and said no.

"Well, Greg...Ms. Reeves...she's...she's gone. She took her life. This happened about six months ago, while you were still in Idaho, Greg. I'm so sorry."

I fell to my knees and started to cry. The brisk ocean breeze was sending chills down my back. All I could hear was Emma saying, "It's okay, it's okay." My face was in my hands, and I didn't want to look up. I felt depleted, like my heart was ripped out of my chest. It didn't feel real. It was heart wrenching.

I was in utter shock and devastation. I had no idea. Nobody told me. Not my family, friends, or the school. But they all knew. Ms. Reeves meant everything to me at McKinney High. She was the one I would have daily talks with about our constant battle with depression. I knew she was depressed, but I didn't think it would come to this. I thought I would be the one to be gone if anything, not her. I saw her as a role model, an influence, and a supportive friend.

I will never forget the feeling that I had when I received this news. It was absolutely brutal, and it hit home for me. I could relate so much to it that it hurt immensely. It took a big toll on me because of how close I was to taking my own life. It was special how we would talk every day and support each other. I was looking forward to meeting up with her and running into each other's arms and having long talks again, but about good things, about how things had changed for the better. I was excited to tell her about the good times at Key Ridge, and that I had made it, that I had overcome my darkest times and extreme depression. This is something I was looking forward to for months. And now I received this news of all things. I couldn't believe Ms. Reeves was gone forever. I couldn't believe she took her own precious life. I knew her well compared to many other people, and she was close enough with me to tell me the struggles in her personal life. But still, I saw her as such a strong, brilliant woman who was able to overcome anything. And I simply could not believe this devastating news. It was shocking, and it hit me like a brick wall. Being in the same boat as her in regards to battling depression made us that much closer. And once I found out that she took her own life, I was absolutely devastated. This was very hard for me to deal with, and finding out about it months after everyone else certainly made me more upset.

As I later grew more accustomed that this actually had happened and gained acceptance, I began reflecting and thinking. I wasn't mad at her for doing this. I didn't think of it as selfish, though some people might. She was facing a major personal battle. She was putting on a fake smile every day and pretending like life was okay. But in reality, nothing was okay. She was trying to defeat depression. Ms. Reeves may have felt like this was the best choice for her situation, which was the saddest realization if it was true.

I knew this because of our daily talks and how we were in the same boat. I knew exactly how she felt. She couldn't escape the dark times, the overwhelming sadness, and the constant struggle each day. She tried to look at things positively and would use teaching as therapy, but her emotions would just fall back to sadness. I was exactly the same way, so I knew how she felt. What I didn't know was that it would come to this. I sincerely thought she would make it through. I was confident in her and her capability to rebound. She was done with living life miserably and having depression as the primary force. I was the same way, and that is why I understand. I was contemplating suicide for two straight years of my life, with many thoughts each and every day of ending the pain and discomfort under my control. If it weren't for Key Ridge, who knows where I would be? We will never know.

All I do know is that that day was one of the most painful and shocking days I have ever experienced. Ms. Reeves meant a lot to me. I will always remember her for the strong, charismatic woman she was and as a dear friend.

19

A Life-Changing Choice

By early February, I was five foot ten and weighed in at 205 pounds. Pure fat. No muscle. I had gotten really big, about forty pounds overweight. Perhaps the sadness following the news about Ms. Reeves took its toll on me. I was still on antidepressants. I still didn't have many friends. I was finding it difficult to branch out, due to not being in school while everyone else still was. They were all finishing senior year while I was at home each day. I didn't belong to clubs or any organizations. Sometimes I would hang out with Isaac and his friends, but that was about it. When a couple of my friends from Key Ridge would have visits, we would hang out.

Cameron had a visit back home to Southern California. He was home visiting from Key Ridge for a week, so I told him we would meet up. One evening, I picked him up from his house, and we drove all the way to downtown LA with a couple of his high school friends. These kids were very sketchy and caused me to feel uneasy. It was good catching up with Cameron, but I still didn't fully enjoy myself given the situation. I was the only one who drove a car, so we went downtown to just check out the city. Once we were finished hanging out, we hopped back in the car, and we were on our way to take Cameron and his two friends home. They were blasting rap music to the fullest volume in my car. I was pretending that I was having fun and okay with it, even though I wasn't. I just went along with it, pretending not to care. They were being distracting and physically bouncing up and down aggressively in their seats.

I glanced back for about a second to see what they were doing. *Boom.* The next thing I saw was the rear end of an SUV smashed into the head of my compact car. I sat there in shock for about ten seconds before I saw the driver open his door and approach my car. I opened my door, and he looked at me like I was a eighteen-year-old clueless piece of shit. He was in his early sixties, and so was his wife. I was rattled by what I just did, and all I could do at the moment was repeatedly apologize. I got the paperwork from the glove compartment, and we exchanged information. Luckily, our vehicles were on the right-hand side of the road and not blocking any traffic. His car had some minor damage, but nothing compared to mine. My car was nearly totaled. He asked me how I managed to crash into him because he was stopped behind traffic at a stoplight. I just told him that I wasn't paying attention and that I had looked back for a split second, and then it was too late. I felt humiliated and ashamed.

When I called my parents from the scene and told them what happened, they were very upset at me. My mom and dad drove to the scene to help me get the situation resolved. I felt awful about what I did. My dad was upset with me and said it was stupid of me for not paying attention on the road, which it was. When we took my car to the shop, they first thought it was totaled. However, once they started working on it, they managed to fix it completely and get it back to normal. It cost a lot of money and inconvenience. After that night, I never once saw Cameron or his friends again. I still haven't seen him to this day. It wasn't just because of the car accident. But they were using me, and I knew they were bad news. They were into drugs, gangs, and getting into trouble. I never participated in drugs or gangs myself, but I put myself in that risky scene by hanging out with them. Originally, I put up with it because I wanted people to hang out with. Cameron was always a fun kid to be around at Key Ridge, but he could never get past old habits. Eventually, I chose to separate myself from that behavior. He also didn't really care about the car crash at all, and neither did his friends. They kind of laughed it off and went about their nights. I saw this as a point to move on and let the negativity from them go.

About a week later, my dad sat me down to have a private talk with me. I knew this was going to be serious. He said that he was proud of how far I had come in my year at Key Ridge, but he still was noticing too many red flags in my behavior. I had just gotten into a careless car wreck, still wasn't able to expand my social network, and was gaining even more weight. So he suggested I start working out and running miles on an outdoor track each day. I took his word and created a workout plan. After a short while, I surprisingly felt healthier each time I would go running. I took this talk very seriously because I had felt like I had already disappointed my father so much in my life and also had cost him lots of money. I felt terrible, and I wanted to change and improve. So whenever I was alone, I began thinking, "What can I do to become a better son and a happier person?"

The running was helping slowly, but I knew there was more out there that could be done than that. The depression was still present, and out of anything in the world, I wanted that to be gone. So the first thing I came up with was that it was time to get rid of the toxic people in my life. I had recently done that with Cameron, and my old high school friends many months ago, but it was time to expand that. During my year at Key Ridge, those people were the only friends I knew. But now, it was different. In just a few months, I would be on my way to college somewhere, which is always a great opportunity to meet new people and have a fresh start. So I just started separating myself from negative influences, including every single Key Ridge person except for one: Mitchell, a kid two years younger than me, and ironically he was from Simi Valley. He was the one who went to Key Ridge and was two houses down from me in Cabin 4. I always played sports with him but never became that close with him until after we both graduated. We started to hang out a lot back home. I knew he was a better influence than a lot of the other kids because he was doing all the right things, like applying to colleges and living closely with his family. He and I were the only two people that applied to universities out of anyone I had met in my year at Key Ridge.

I noticed that my choice was helping. Now I had a few really close friends: Mitchell, Isaac, Ashley, and a couple others. I realized that having a few close friends at the time was a better trade-off for me than having a lot of acquaintances because these close friends were trustworthy and caring about our friendships. And I needed that at the time.

But as I began to contemplate my personal well-being even more, some thoughts came into my head that made me especially curious. I began writing everything down about the medications I was taking. I wanted to keep track of every little detail because it had the possibility to be life changing. So I started to write down the details:

I was taking two antidepressant medications. They

were meant to help people manage their depression and anxiety and make them stable. By this point, I had been on them for over two full years continuously, nonstop. Some of my psychologists thought I had situational depression while others believed it to be permanent. Ever since I was on the meds, I became very overweight. And the most critical point of all: every time that I attempted suicide or was in my darkest depression, I was still taking the meds.

I took all these facts into consideration, and I began thinking about my options. All I wanted was to be happy and content with myself permanently. I didn't want to have to take medications for the rest of my life. I didn't want a pill defining my lifestyle and who I was. I certainly didn't want people at college knowing that I took them, such as my future, soon-to-be college roommate.

I told myself that it might be time to be a risk-taker. And then after pondering the idea for a long time, the final decision was made. I was going to wean myself off the medications without medical supervision.

It is pretty obvious that nobody is ever supposed to do this and that it could be extremely detrimental and cause even more intense suicidal thoughts in some cases. But my reasoning was that I didn't have much to lose, especially because my lowest McKinney points were while I was taking the medications. I thought this was very suspicious, and it made me not trust the meds working in my body. I knew they worked for other people, but I felt they were not working for me. I wanted a change. I didn't want to be on these medications any longer. Nobody thought I could handle life without the meds, but I believed. So there you have it, an eighteen-year-old kid who just left rehab for depression was now weaning off antidepressant medications unsupervised in hopes of being fully cleansed.

I took them morning and night, so to start the process, I decided to cut the morning pills in half and keep the night ones at the full dosage. I did this for two weeks. After the two weeks, I felt the same. No better, no worse. Just about average. But I decided to sit down with my dad and tell him what I was doing. I didn't want anyone else to know. Not my family or friends and certainly not my psychiatrist. When I told my dad, I expected him to be worried and angry with me, but thought maybe he would offer some good advice.

What I didn't expect was what he actually told me. So when I first said to him that I was slowly weaning myself off my antidepressant medications, a small smile grew on his face. He said, "Son, believe it or not, I was going to suggest this in the coming months. I know it isn't necessarily the right or healthiest thing to do, but given your circumstances, it could be worth the try. I know you don't want to be on these meds forever, especially with big things like college coming up. But the thing that makes this come to my mind is that your most severe feelings of suicide were while you were taking these meds, so do they really even work that well for you? I know you don't want to be on these pills forever, right, Greg?"

My mouth nearly dropped in utter shock and appreciation. My dad and I were on the same page, which was bizarre considering how risky it was. We had in-depth talks about how this should be taken seriously and how it could possibly make me even more depressed or irrational, though we thought that was unlikely. So my dad and I tracked what I was doing very closely. Every little change would be documented. Only he and I knew about this. If we told anyone else, it would all come crashing down. But it was a risk that I was willing to take, and so was he. My dad wanted to see his son in full happiness and control of his life, not monitored by some pills that I put in my mouth each day. And we knew the psychiatrist would not approve of giving me less dosage. So we decided to go for it ourselves.

On the third week of the weaning process, my dad and I concluded that I should start cutting my pills in the mornings and nights, instead of just the mornings. We would talk in private about how I was feeling about three times per day, to make sure I was remaining stable. After two weeks of doing this new tactic, I was still doing fine. I saw minimal improvements, but no setbacks, which was good. The main improvement I noticed is that I lost six pounds that month. It was probably a combination of running each day and weaning off the meds, but even still, I was very excited to see that progress.

After the first month, I began to take the next step and completely stop taking my morning dosage. I would just take my meds that I cut at night. This lasted two weeks as well. I started feeling a little bit happier more often, which was an interesting result.

During this time, I was also attending a local community college. I was just taking two classes: psychology and journalism. My dad thought it was a good idea for me to get accustomed to college courses and get a feel for how a college lifestyle would be. It was also good for me to be independent, get out of the house a bit, and meet new people of all different ages and backgrounds.

One day, I came home from my run that afternoon on the track. I was exhausted and drenched in sweat but feeling good. My mom was in the kitchen doing dishes. When I entered the door to the house, she looked over with this glow in her eyes and a charming smile. "Greg, you have some mail," she said, in a jittery voice. I walked over and was so curious, just by how bubbly and excited she was. I opened the envelope, and I read these words out loud: "Congratulations on your admittance to the University of Arizona!"

My hands began to sweat. My heart began to race. And my smile turned as big as it may have ever gotten. I had just been accepted into the University of Arizona. I was beside myself because it felt surreal, almost too good to be true. It didn't really make sense to me. For the past couple years, I had been suffocated by depression and people constantly telling me that I should never go to college. That I'd never make it, and if I did, I wouldn't survive for very long. People said I wouldn't be able to handle it and that I shouldn't even bother pursuing college because of my depression. But here I was; I had just been accepted to the University of Arizona, and I had heard some absolutely amazing things about that school.

My mom, dad, and brother were all very proud of me. I think they were almost in too much shock to believe it. We were expecting some small school acceptances but we thought it would be a long shot for such a big and well-known university. It was almost a feeling of, "Is this really happening right now?" It had been years since they had seen me truly happy, and in this moment I was ecstatic.

A little over a week later, I was completely off my anti-depressant medications, still unsupervised by medical doctors. In a week and a half, my mom scheduled a psychiatrist appointment for me since I was just about due for one. So that meant I had a week and a half to see how my body would react without having any medications for the first time in over two years. I kept up my routine of working out, not only to lose weight and to feel good but also to cleanse my body of the medications that were still left in my system due to the accumulation over time.

A week and a half went by. Nothing dramatic happened. I continued attending my community college classes and working out. My emotional state was stable, considering the circumstances. There were no signs of depression, anxiety, suicidal thoughts, or anything slightly irrational for that matter. It was the day of the appointment with my psychiatrist, because he wanted to check up on me and see if I needed a refill for my medications.

My mom, dad, brother, and I sat down in my psychiatrist's office. He began by asking me questions revolving around my feelings and my depression symptoms. I told him there were none. He then asked, "How are the medications treating you? Do you need any more?"

My dad interrupted. "Do you know what, Doctor?" I cut my dad off that instant. I knew he was going to lay it all out there for him to hear. He went silent after I cut him off though. I took a deep sigh and prepared to break the news to the doctor as well as my mom and brother right then and there.

"Doctor, I need to tell you something."

"What is it?" they all asked.

"I know this is going to come as a surprise, but I am completely off my antidepressants. I stopped taking my meds."

My mom's eyes grew to the size of golf balls, and her mouth dropped. My brother looked up at me, confused. The doctor was in disbelief. He asked, "Greg, so you're telling me that you went off the medications by yourself?"

"Yes, I weaned myself off them and monitored it with my dad," I responded.

The doctor looked at me and said, "Do you know

what, kid? I can't help you anymore. If you're going to do this, then you're on your own."

My family and I got up, left his office, and closed the door. That was the end of it with my psychiatrist. When we walked through the parking lot and eventually got into the car, my mom starting ranting and questioning my dad and me. She was questioning why we did this and especially without professional supervision. She said that it could have easily made me more suicidal instead of less. She was upset that she wasn't told about it and that we were not obeying the doctor's orders. We sympathized with her, and both my dad and I understood where my mom was coming from.

But I explained to her that this was different. Normally, I live by honesty and trustworthiness. But this was my health and future at stake. I explained to her that the medications made me fat. I explained how I was self-conscious about other people knowing that I take them. I told her how I simply despised taking them each morning and night. And last but most important, I made sure it was clear that each one of my suicide attempts happened while I was taking the antidepressant medications. I seriously was skeptical whether they actually worked or not. The meds had not brought one proof-positive thing to my life. My dad and I were able to put the pieces together. But throughout this entire time of trying to talk with different doctors about allowing me to get off the medications, they seemed to just not get the hint and seemed like meds were the best thing for me. A few doctors even said that I would be on them for life. Some thought it was permanent depression rather than situational depression. But I didn't want any depression anymore, nor did I want any meds to be relied upon. And at the end of the day, I feel that I am in control of what I put into my body. And I made all this clear to my mom, brother, and extended family, that this was why I decided to take the risk of weaning off unsupervised. My father agreed and was there for support and guidance.

It took a few days for this to sink into my mom's head. She used to agree with the doctors that I may have had to be on medications for life, so this came as a big surprise to her. But when she thought about it more in depth and analyzed the situation, she came to terms and actually became content with the situation. Her son was no longer on antidepressant medications. My life didn't revolve around a pill anymore. That was huge. Yes, it was risky, but this turned out to be one of the most significant and positive decisions that I would ever make in my life thus far. It has been an absolutely life-changing choice still to this day.

20

Gearing up for College

It was the middle of spring semester at the community college I was attending. I was continuing to take journalism and psychology to prepare me for the transition between Key Ridge and a real university. I was doing well in these two classes and actually really enjoyed them both. I also seemed to be enjoying not being on the medications. As each week went by, it seemed as if I was becoming more stable and becoming myself again. My family and I took a trip out to Tucson, Arizona, to visit the University of Arizona. On the flight over, I was nervous because I knew this could be my future. It would be a huge jump going from a place like Key Ridge to the University of Arizona, which is home to approximately forty thousand students. We had a great tour of the campus and facilities. In just one day around Tucson, my heart became filled with joy.

I loved the beautiful campus with the old redbrick buildings. It was very peaceful and serene. The classrooms and facilities appeared to be very impressive. The basketball and football stadiums were astonishing due to the tradition and success the Arizona Wildcats athletics program had had over time. I loved the college-town feel. The entire city essentially depends on the U of A because there is no professional sports teams or an abundance of other activities that a large city would offer. Everywhere you went something is related to U of A, and someone told you to "Bear Down," as that is the school motto. The warm weather was great, the people seemed friendly, and the girls had me wide-eyed by how beautiful they were, especially coming from Key Ridge. The school spirit was in full force no matter where you went. The Greek life was strong I had heard, and the school had over five hundred clubs and activities to be a part of. The recreational center is ranked as one of the best overall in the country. It is absolutely amazing. The student union was full of many great eateries and other resources.

As we concluded the tour, our guide took us to the Eller College of Management. This was the business college at the university, consisting of nine different majors. Eller has a high reputation, as it is ranked the number tenth best undergraduate public business school nationally, according to *U.S. News and World Report*. This was an important part of the tour because I was considering declaring my major as pre-business for my freshman year. This meant that I had to take all the prerequisite business and general education classes first. Then at the end of sophomore year or beginning of junior year, I would apply to Eller if I had a high enough GPA, among many other required qualifications. I was determined to work hard early in my collegiate academic career in hopes to one day become a student of the Eller College of Management.

Although it was a little bit intimidating and nerve-racking being on a college that big with entirely new people, I still had a gut feeling that this place was the right one for me. When I returned home to Simi Valley, I officially committed to the University of Arizona, and I was beyond excited to be a Wildcat.

In the meantime I was using the two community college classes as preparation for what the big university was holding for me in the near future. It was an exciting time for me because I felt like I was making big strides in my life. I was off my medications for good, I was going to a community college, and I had just been accepted to the U of A and committed! This was March 2012, and I soon began looking for a college roommate for freshman year beginning in August.

I used a suggested website called Room Surf to look for prospects. Room Surf is meant for roommate matching based on common interests, hobbies, and other factors that play a role in living situations for freshman entering college. A guy by the name of Patrick messaged me, and we began talking with one another, our priorities, and what dorms we wanted to live in, etc. It seemed like he was a good guy who liked a lot of the same things that I did. We would talk every now and then to get to know each other better, and although he was a complete stranger, I felt like he could be a realistic option for my freshman year roommate in the dorms. I was already used to living with roommates at Key Ridge, so it wasn't a huge change for me. But it was important to find a good, trustworthy roommate, someone who I could become friends with and engage in a social life with in the college environment.

By now it was time to do two things: select a dorm and reserve an orientation date. I went on the website and checked out all the dorm options, which took a while because there were something like twenty-four dorms on campus. I checked out all the details, prices, amenities, and locations of the dorms. I even watched virtual tours of each one to give me a better perspective on what it would be like. My top choices were all located on the same street on campus, and I ranked my top three in relation to what Patrick wanted. As I began to talk with Patrick more, I learned more about him. It turned out he was from Chicago and was a die-hard fan of the Chicago sports teams. He was very excited to be at U of A, similar to everyone who comes to the school. It sounded like we had some common interests, including sports, socializing with friends, and working out. He said that his top dorm choice was the one that I chose first, too. Once we found out that we both wanted the same one, it kind of clicked, and we started the talk of submitting the official roommate application. A couple weeks later and after some more conversations through Room Surf, social media, and text, we both decided that we wanted to officially become roommates. The only thing holding us back was whether or not we both got in to our top dorm choice. Soon enough, we received confirmation that we both indeed were accepted into residency of our top dorm choice and would be roommates! We were beyond excited, and it was a big relief. Knowing that we would be roommates, we set up our orientations to be on the same exact day so we could meet each other in person before college move-in day. The orientation day was set for June 6, 2012, just two months before we would step foot on campus to officially begin our collegiate careers.

The spring semester was now over, and I was very content with how things panned out. I received an *A* in my psychology class and a *B* in my journalism class. This was good in the mind of my parents, considering I was at Key Ridge not long ago. The schooling at Key Ridge was much more accommodating, and the difficulty was somewhat toned down compared to that of a regular high school such as McKinney in Simi Valley. I also continued to work out on the track about five days a week. I would run three miles and also watch what I ate. I lost twenty pounds in just over four months. But the most significant thing was that I just felt happier. I was now a couple months completely off the antidepressants, and I was doing great. There were no signs of depression or anxiety. In fact, I was happy very consistently, almost all the time. The combination of being off the meds, doing well in community college classes, and gearing up for the University of Arizona in August were good signs of improvement.

As college became closer and much more of a reality, I had nearly cut off almost every single old Key Ridge contact. I did this not because they were bad people but because they may not have been the best people to have in my life at that moment. I had already lost contact with Cameron. I still contacted Peyton and a couple other guys in Timber every now and then, but it was rarely. The only person who I regularly talked with was Mitchell. At the beginning when I first left Key Ridge, I would write them letters every week, and they would write me back. But with time, our relationships were dwindling. In a way, it was sad to see. These guys helped change my life, no doubt. They were there for me when I was down, and we would spend twenty-four seven, three sixty-five together. Literally.

But this was over a half-year later, and I was starting to become a different person. I was striving for improvement, self-development, and happiness. And although I enjoyed being around my friends while at Key Ridge, some of them wouldn't do me any good if we were friends in the real world because of the negative trends they would carry with them. And this was not the fault of Key Ridge. Key Ridge does a spectacular job in developing people to improve their lives, but it only truly helps the kids who are open and willing for help. Unfortunately, some of the kids do not fully commit to improving and taking control of their lives, which makes for a rough transition back into the real world once their time at Key Ridge comes to an end.

This was not easy at all. I missed these guys because of how close we were in that one year, but I knew it was better for me if I distanced myself. I tried to keep in touch with the staff members who I was close with at Key Ridge, as we had some great relationships, and many of them helped change my life as well. But the bottom line is that I knew I shouldn't live in the Key Ridge bubble forever. It was time for me to move on to bigger and better opportunities. So as of the summer before college, I would only talk to one student from Key Ridge regularly, and that was Mitchell. We continued hanging out more and grew to become closer friends then what we were at Key Ridge. We played basketball often, went out to eat, and his family would have me over for dinner. His family was very nice, and I trusted Mitchell because of his relationship with them. He had also completely reshaped his life.

One day, Mitchell and I had finished playing basketball at a local park. There was no one really there besides us. We began talking about the past and about our experiences at Key Ridge. The reflection is always crazy to talk about, from going to rock bottom to where we both were now. We talked about our old friends back in Idaho and where people were at in life. Just a couple months prior, our good friend from Idaho had tragically passed away. I was friends with him during my time at Key Ridge as he was on most of the all-star teams with me. But he and Mitchell were very, very close. It was very sad for me but even more so for Mitchell. He was a great kid, with an uplifting personality. Unfortunately, he could not overcome the struggle with drugs that he was dealing with.

Mitchell and I were sitting there trying to think of all the Key Ridge people who "made it." Then we started talking about college because I was already committed to the University of Arizona and he was committed to a great university in Southern California. Then a thought popped into my mind, so I turned to him and asked him a question. "Hey, man, who else do we know from Key Ridge who made it to a four-year university?" We sat there silent for about a minute, thinking and trying to mumble some names. I thought of one girl who was going to a local community college. And he thought of one that was possibly going to UC Merced, but Mitchell was unsure if she actually attended. There was one statement to be made, and it still blows my mind to this day: Mitchell and I are two of the only people we went to school with at Key Ridge who successfully made it to a four-year university that we know of. That means that there were essentially two people out of a couple hundred who would go on to a university that we knew of.

A lot of people leave Key Ridge and begin community college while working at a local store or restaurant. Some go to trade school, or strive for other intriguing endeavors. These kids are off to a great start, better than most, and I hope that one day these people can seek even bigger aspirations to lead to happiness and success. But it was hard to believe that Mitchell and I were the only two people that we were sure of attending a university. It was an eye-opener. Imagine if you only had two people from your high school graduating class going on to attend a four-year university. That is a crazy thought. It made me feel that I was on a pathway to success and also proved the fact right that it was a good idea to let go of most of my old Key Ridge friends.

On June 6, 2012, my family and I woke up eager for our flight to Tucson, Arizona. It was orientation day, which meant that I got a more in-depth tour of campus, selected my classes for fall semester, got a chance to meet some fellow students, and would finally meet my future roommate in person. I was anxious for this because I was really banking on Patrick being a good, fun person to live with. My family and I flew into the airport, drove a rental car to campus, and stepped foot on a lively but chaotic atmosphere. There were people everywhere, with parents and families. The students were all very excited, but we all seemed to be like lost puppies on a large campus and a completely new situation. But orientation turned out to be a lot of fun and very informative. I learned a lot about the pre-business major and how the process works in regards to applying for Eller in the future. I learned about the rich, diverse history of the school as well as the limitless opportunities the school offers for students to get involved in.

At lunchtime, I finally met up with Patrick for the first time. He was a tall kid with an athletic build. His family and my family all sat down for lunch in the student union to get to know each other. We all seemed to hit it off pretty well, and he seemed like a great future roommate. The next day my family and I flew back to Simi Valley, and I felt overwhelmed with excitement on becoming an Arizona Wildcat. The orientation visit was great overall, and I was relieved to meet Patrick in person instead of relying on social media until move-in day.

In late July, my family and I took a ten-day vacation, as this would be the last time we would spend time together before moving me out to college. We had a great trip, and it was relaxing and good for me to clear my mind before starting an entirely new chapter of my life—college. I was going to miss my parents and Josh very much, so it was very good to have one last summer vacation together before my freshman year.

21

The Next Two Years

It was August 20, 2012. I was moving away to college. I had never thought those words would ever surface from my mouth, nor did anybody else. But it was happening, and I just had to go for it. My family and I flew to Tucson for the move-in and the transition to college. When we arrived, we rented a car and went straight to Bed Bath & Beyond to pick up my college move-in package. It was basically a giant package of all the essentials I would need for my dorm: bedding, storage containers, and hygiene. Everything else either came already furnished or Patrick and I were planning on bringing in, such as the television. It was very hectic moving in because freshman students were doing the same exact thing with their parents, so it was quite congested. But within two days, both Patrick and I were officially moved in and ready to go. I said bye to my parents and Josh. And let me tell you that was not easy. It was almost like the good-bye to my family as the bodyguard took me away to Key Ridge. But this was on a much, much better note. The four of us hugged each other good-bye.

Before they left, I looked each one of them in the eyes and told them how thankful I was to have them in my life. I said that if it weren't for them I would not be at the University of Arizona. I thanked my dad for pushing me and never giving up on me. I thanked my brother for being my best friend, and I told him to keep working hard in school. I was a bit nervous for him because this was going to be his first year at McKinney High School, and we all knew how my experience went. I was hoping that he would have a positive experience with many great friends. He was planning to play soccer, so I wished him the absolute best and told him I was always here if he needed any guidance or a person to talk to. I thanked my mom for being the gracious person that she was and for always being so caring and helpful toward our family. Although I would see my family in a few months for Thanksgiving, it felt weird. It felt painful to let them go. But before they left, I told them that I was sorry for what I did in high school, and I promised that I would work hard in college to become a better person and student. We said our good-byes and wished each other the best and expressed our love. Finally, they made their way to the car and drove to their hotel. Although I was ecstatic to be at college, I was saddened by the good-bye to my family. I could tell they were excited for me but also very nervous because I feel like they didn't fully trust me yet after my rough past couple of years.

By then I had no choice but to get adapted to the college lifestyle. My family was gone, and I felt like it was just me going for this whole new experience. Patrick and I seemed to get along very well from the start, which was great. We would work out together, play basketball, go get meals, and meet new people in our dorm.

In my first week on campus, I felt two things: great excitement and nervousness. The excitement was obvious. But the nervousness stemmed from the feeling that I was behind everybody else on a social level. I felt like I was playing catch up. Everyone on campus seemed to be very natural when it came to his or her social behavior. Also, the girls seemed to be very pretty, which was definitely something that I wasn't used to because I wasn't even allowed to interact with any girls for an entire year. I was kind of shy and closed up during the first week on campus because it was intimidating. I kept an open mind, but I just felt like that everyone else was simply better than me and more used to this type of social environment.

But as each day went by, I grew a little bit more comfortable with the situation. I would meet a couple new people each day, which was exciting. The dorm was very social and helped break me out of my shell a little bit. By then school had already started, and things seemed to be going fine. I was in five classes, and the professors seemed good. It was a significant step up from Key Ridge though, so I did my best to adapt. The classes were larger, and everything was a huge step up. It was not a cakewalk anymore, and it was time for me to start off my collegiate career strong, with dedication.

When I came home from school one day during the first week, Patrick was sitting in our dorm room. And just a few seconds after I walked in he asked, "Greg, do you plan on rushing?" I hardly even knew what that meant, but I assumed it had something to do with a fraternity. I responded, "No, I don't. Do you?" Patrick then said, "Maybe. I don't really know yet, but I'm considering it." He then told me that his friend who was a sophomore at the time invited him to one of his own fraternity's events. "Do you want to come with and check it out?" his friend asked Patrick. "My friend's fraternity is having a casual event at the minor-league baseball game tonight, and he wanted to know if we wanted to join. What do you say, Greg?"

I was very hesitant, but I said, "Sure." So that evening, Patrick and I showed up at his friend's fraternity house. There were a lot of guys in the house, and we made some casual conversations with a few to get a vibe for the whole thing. We then took several cars and drove to watch the game. It was a good time and was interesting meeting so many new people at once. They seemed to be pretty down to earth, close with one another, and I could tell they were proud and loved being in their fraternity.

Later that evening, Patrick and I returned to the dorm. He told me that he was now definitely going to register for fraternity recruitment. I was a little more optimistic but still somewhat hesitant. But I knew that even if I rushed some fraternities, that wouldn't lock me into joining one necessarily. I could always back out of the process if I wanted to. So I decided to call my parents and make them aware of the situation. They were against it and thought it would distract me from getting off to a good start in school. I couldn't disagree. But it was only a twenty-five-dollar fee to participate in fraternity recruitment, and even if I was to be selected to join one, there was no obligation to. Although not thrilled, my parents gave me the okay to go through rushing the fraternities.

Recruitment was during the third week of school, during the evenings from Monday all the way through Friday. Each person was allowed to choose the houses that they wanted to check out. The more houses you visited, the better chances you had in getting selected to be a part of a fraternity. There were about twenty fraternities on campus, and I chose to rush six of them. Each one presented a different vibe. But at most of the houses, I felt that they had too many members, some even on the higher end of 150 boys.

But the last house I visited on that Monday really drew my attention. It was a huge house, with a very old, rustic feel. It felt the most like a home. Someone took me on a tour of the house, and I was surprised to see that there were twenty-four bedrooms in the house. The front yard was full of grass and nearly three-quarters of a football field in length. The backyard was gigantic and even had a sand volleyball court and basketball court. One thing that I noticed was that there weren't a hundred or two hundred guys in the house. There seemed to be only about twenty, which was extremely small. And the reason for that was because this was their first semester returning to campus. They were looking for people who wanted to take the opportunity to help bring the fraternity up from nearly scratch. As I talked with a handful of the guys, I seemed to be more comfortable than when talking to guys in other houses. I felt like I was being myself, and everyone seemed to be very relaxed and genuine. I left the house around 9:00 p.m. that evening thinking, "This has to be my top option so far."

The week went by, and I started narrowing down my options. I kept getting callbacks, which was a necessity because it had to be a mutual fit in order to pledge a fraternity. I had to select that I wanted to return to that fraternity the following day, and they had to review me and select that they even wanted me to return themselves. And there seemed to be that connection.

Thursday was preference dinner, which is the last step before receiving a bid from a fraternity. I made it to preference dinner of my favorite house. Zero out of the other five fraternities that I rushed called me back for preference dinner, just the one. At preference dinner, I just tried to meet as many people as I could and to present myself with a good image. This was the last night of voting, so I was really hoping that I would be selected because I enjoyed each time that I was there.

It was late Friday night, and I was waiting around for a phone call, hoping that it was one of the guys calling to offer me a bid. Patrick was also waiting around. He had a couple of other fraternities as his priorities.

It turned out that both of us got bids from separate fraternities, neither being the one that hosted us for the baseball game. I had received an offer to join my favorite one, and I was filled with excitement. I was shocked because I went from not wanting to rush at all to actually receiving an offer to join my favorite fraternity. So the next morning before class, I called my parents and now told them of this situation. I was scared of this conversation, assuming they'd shut down the idea of joining a fraternity. And I was right. They were happy for me that I got an offer but were dead set against it. They thought it would be a major distraction and said it would end up being more money than expected. I understood their point. But I told them that I understood that school is first priority and that I would stay diligent on my schoolwork. I expressed to them how positive I felt about this fraternity and how this could be a very special opportunity, especially because I'd be helping with the reestablishment on campus. They liked the idea of that and also how it wasn't hundreds of guys. Instead, there were only about twenty.

My parents said they wanted to think on it and talk it over and that they would call me back later that afternoon. So I went to class and eagerly went through my day, as I could only think about that phone call and their final decision. Around four, I got a call from my dad. In a monotone voice, he said, "Greg, you can join. Just remember that school is first. And make sure to not do anything stupid. If you don't want to continue pledging the fraternity, you can always drop out at any point. And if I hear about your grades slacking, you're done with the fraternity. No ifs, ands, or buts."

I probably said thank you ten different times on that call, and I was so excited. I kept reassuring him that even though it could be a risky decision to join a fraternity due to many obligations during my freshman year of college, I could handle it. I told him how I had a great gut feeling about it and how all the guys were nice and friendly. I just had a feeling that this fraternity was the right choice.

So I was now an official part of the fraternity, and there were fifteen other guys in the new fall 2012 pledge class with me. This made for thirty-five guys total. Even just a few weeks in, I was so confident that this was going to be a terrific decision. I grew to be very close friends with the guys, and we did many fun activities that first semester, including camping, sporting events, serenade dances for the sororities, and most important, our rechartering ceremony. This rechartering officially gave our chapter full recognition from the university and the fraternity national office. During that first semester, I really learned to come out of my shell. I became less shy. In fact, I grew to become pretty outgoing, even just that first semester.

There was one time where a handful of us sat down together and talked about our pasts, more specifically our life stories. I was scared as hell to share mine. At this point only my family and my old Key Ridge friends knew about my past. But we all agreed to share in full honesty. This was a breakthrough point for me because I really became content and accepted the situation that I could not change my past. In fact, some of the guys even said they gained more respect for me after hearing about my story than before they knew any details about me. It was a special moment for me, and I treasured that they cared enough to listen while promising to tell nobody else.

As the semester progressed, I became very outgoing and sincerely happy with my choice and my life. In November 2012 I finished pledging and was officially initiated into the fraternity as an active brother. This was even more special because all of us were considered Refounding Fathers because we helped with the reestablishment of the fraternity back onto the U of A campus.

Although I was very busy each day with the fraternity, I finished my first semester of college with a 3.67 GPA. My parents were very proud of me, and to be honest I was proud of myself. I think I kind of surprised myself and definitely surprised my parents. It's almost as if they didn't expect me to have success right away at a large university and getting used to a new lifestyle, coming out of Key Ridge so recently. But I did it, and I wasn't looking back.

I am now, as of this writing, twenty-three years old and a senior at the University of Arizona. These have been the best four years of my life. I feel that I have worked my absolute hardest not only in school but personally as well. While working hard, I have had tons of fun and have matured along the way. I just finished my third year in a row of living in the fraternity house. That was also one of the best choices I have ever made. The combination of the U of A and the fraternity have given me so many wonderful friends, memories, and unforgettable experiences. From going to almost every U of A basketball and football game, to rock-climbing mountains, to going on weekend trips, to celebrating our twenty-first birthdays in Vegas, to spring break vacations, to sitting back just hanging out with a couple close friends, and infinite more memories and good times. One of the most special things that have happened to me in the fraternity is that I have received three "little brothers." Each semester, the new members are given an older member to be their "big brother." This process happens through mutual selection, so the new member has to select the current fraternity member and vice versa for it to happen. I have been blessed with three little brothers who I have grown very close with.

And the plethora of Arizona Wildcats basketball and football games I have been to has shaped my career as a college student. I am a die-hard fan of our sports teams. I have only missed a couple home basketball and football games in my entire four years as a student so far. The student section is lively and even won "Best Student Section in the Nation" when I was a junior. We are usually one of the nation's best teams in basketball, and our football program is on the rise, so it is a great time to be a student. I am forever grateful for my choice to attend the University of Arizona and join my fraternity as well. I have become an entirely different person than I was in high school. Instead of being depressed, negative, and hopeless, I am now happy, confident, and motivated. Much credit goes to my fraternity brothers for really helping me break out of my shell, in which I was closed-up and shy before that.

My freshman and sophomore years of college were fantastic. I had met so many uplifting people around campus and had joined some fun clubs and organizations outside of the fraternity as well. I joined a self-development organization. This is where I would eventually meet my mentor. He and I grew close, and in fact, my mentor was the very first person I ever told about writing this book.

I had worked hard throughout my first two years of

school, putting myself in a good position by the time it was time for me to apply to the Eller College of Management at the beginning of junior year. This was a big deal because Eller is a highly ranked business school and difficult to get in to. The average GPA for applicants is a 3.5. I had to select my major preferences, submit a cover letter, update my resume, pass an entrance exam, and pass an extensive interview. If I did all of that, then I would be accepted into Eller. The process took over a month from start to finish.

It was October 14, 2014, which was family weekend at the University of Arizona. My family was in town visiting me, and I was showing Josh the ropes of how the college lifestyle goes. They flew into Tucson the day before, and we had already had a fun twenty-four hours together. But later in the evening, I received an e-mail to my student account and the subject line read, "Eller College of Management — Acceptance Status."

The moment of truth was lying beneath a click of a button. I either got in or I didn't. I opened the e-mail with my mom, dad, and brother by my side. "Dear Greg, Congratulations on your acceptance into the Eller College of Management with a major in marketing!"

I literally leaped out of my chair and started jumping in pure joy. My mom was screaming in excitement, and my dad and brother were celebrating. It was a memorable moment for me to be accepted into Eller and major in marketing, which was my first priority choice for my major.

This was another turning point for me. It felt like Key Ridge was so far in the past now because I was beginning to accomplish some relevant things in my life. This was a huge step, as this reputable business school would help catapult me into gaining professional experience with internships and jobs.

The first semester was difficult and strenuous. It felt like I was working all the time, but it was worth it. I was determined and just felt truly blessed that I was accepted and had an opportunity as good as this one. I did well my first semester despite the difficulties. I was offered and accepted two internships. The first one was interning for a professional sports team during the summer. And the second one had to do with collegiate athletics for the following school year. Things seemed to be heading in the right direction as I was concluding my junior year.

22

Inexplicable

Thursday, May 14, 2015, people at the University of Arizona had begun packing up for summer vacation. Final exams had already been completed. Usually, I would have been home for summer break already, but I decided to stay on campus until Saturday, May 16 because that was the University of Arizona's graduation ceremony for the seniors. I wanted to be there for three very close friends of mine. My friends Landon and Ivan were fraternity brothers who I had lived with for a couple years. The other one was my friend Jenny, who happened to be my desk assistant in my dorm freshman year. Jenny and I grew close throughout our time in college.

The University of Arizona has two types of graduations. The first is the one for your specific college and major, like business, science, engineering, etc. Then there was the big graduation commencement ceremony where every graduating senior was in attendance. This was taking place Saturday evening in the football stadium. On this day, Thursday, I went to Ivan's graduation with his family and girlfriend. It was a nice ceremony. I was very much looking forward to the big ceremony Saturday night to celebrate everyone graduating. Landon's separate graduation for his major was set for the next day. Jenny's was taking place at 9:00 a.m. on Saturday morning. I was planning to go to Jenny's graduation with my freshman-year roommate, Patrick, as they were very close friends as well.

Earlier Thursday afternoon, I got a text from one of my little brothers in the fraternity, Evan. It read, "Craig, when will you be home so we can say bye for summer break?" Fun fact: Many friends of mine call me Craig instead of Greg as a joke to mess around. Evan used this to his advantage, as he was a very playful guy. So I responded, "Do you want to hang out for a while around 8:00 p.m. tonight?" He said, "Yes, I'll see you at the house then."

Hours went by. I began saying bye to the people who had flights that day. As it approached that evening, my friend Logan told me that he wanted me to go outside to say hello to his dad when he arrived from Phoenix. In the meantime, a few friends and I made margaritas and hung out since it was going to be a few months until seeing each other again. Evan arrived around 8:15. We hung out for a while and drank a couple margaritas together with a few other friends. About an hour later, I took a quick shower because I was going out to the bars to celebrate with a few friends who were graduating. When I was in the shower, Evan shouts, "Craig! Logan's dad is here. Get out of the shower." I quickly got out and went out to the front yard to greet Logan's dad. It was Logan, his father, Evan, and I. We all shared a great, long conversation for about fifteen minutes before Logan and his dad drove back up to Phoenix for the summer. Logan and his dad would see me soon, as I would be relocating to the Phoenix area for my summer internship.

Evan and I walked back to my room, where people were still making margaritas. He said, "Greg, I think I got to head out soon. I have a long drive tomorrow back home to Denver." We said our good-byes for the summer.

I told him to enjoy the summer and that when we come back in August, the next school year would be even better than this year was. We had a blast being big bro and little bro for his first full year. I told him to drive safely and to text me when he got home the next day. The drive from Tucson to Denver takes about twelve hours. He told me that he was planning on leaving early Friday afternoon to get into Denver later that night. Before he walked out the door, I said to him, "Evan, love you man, and I am glad to have you as my little bro. Have a good summer." He responded, "Love you too, Craig. Talk to you soon."

Friday, May 15, 2015, I went to Landon's graduation, which was similar to Ivan's. After that, I began packing up, as I was set to move to Phoenix the following Monday. My dad was driving to Tucson from Simi Valley to help me transition into the new city for the summer. Once I finished packing, I went to sleep because I was waking up early for Jenny's graduation. In the meantime, Evan was on the road making the trip back to Denver.

Saturday, May 16, 2015, Patrick picked me up early in the morning to go grab some Dunkin' Donuts before we drove over to Jenny's graduation. We decided to eat them in the audience of the graduation, and of course, we were the only ones doing that. We were both glad to be there because we knew how happy and proud Jenny was. She had worked so hard throughout all four years of college, and she deserved this more than anyone. She even asked Patrick and I to join her and her family for her graduation brunch following the ceremony. We were all looking forward to that. Her graduation lasted about three hours, and she was scheduled to walk midway through it.

About twenty minutes after Jenny walked up proudly

on that stage to graduate, I felt a buzz from my phone. The update read: "Facebook Notification." I clicked on the notification to see what it was about.

When I finished reading it, I looked over at Patrick with a blank, helpless look. I wasn't even paying attention to the graduation anymore. I showed him the message. He didn't have any words either.

The message was from one of my fraternity brothers, and he sent it out to all the members. It read as follows:

"Hey guys, I don't know if you've heard, but Evan got in a horrible car accident late last night while he was driving back to Colorado. He is currently in surgery and under critical condition. Keep him and his family in your thoughts and prayers."

I told Patrick that we had to leave the graduation and that he needed to drive me home at that moment. He dropped me off, and I said, "Tell Jenny congrats again for me. I wish I could make the brunch, but I can't."

I walked into the fraternity house, headed toward my room, and shut my door. I stared at the wall for about thirty minutes, not knowing what to do. My head was confused, and my heart felt numb. My mind was racing. I took two doses of NyQuil at 1:00 p.m. that day, not because I was tired or sick but because I just wanted to sleep. I dropped to my knees and prayed for Evan to make a healthy recovery. I set my alarm for 5:00 p.m. Then I went to sleep.

The sound of my alarm was going off. It was 5:00 p.m. I went to turn off my alarm. Then I slowly went to unlock my phone, and as I did so, there was another notification. This time the notification read, "You have twenty-eight new messages." I didn't even need to read one message that moment to know what had happened. I fell onto my bed instantly, absolutely distraught. Crying hysterically. Evan had passed away.

When I found out the news, I cannot put into words how I felt. It was inexplicable. I was beyond distraught and could not control my tears. It felt like a part of my heart was ripped out of my chest. I felt sad and hopeless, as did everybody who knew Evan. At about 5:30 p.m., I gained enough courage to open my door and go talk to people in the rest of the fraternity house. And when I did that, every single person was crying. And I mean every single person. People were laying facedown in the front yard, some in their rooms, and others on our rooftop balcony. Just crying. I went on the roof, and everyone was just hugging each other up there, crying on one another's shoulders. Everyone was telling each other "I love you." I called my parents, trying to keep it together, and ended up unleashing in tears over the phone.

A couple hours later, we made a bonfire. In the meantime, Landon and Ivan, as well as some other good friends, had their graduation. I was clearly not going anymore, nor did anyone else because of what had happened. I don't know how they did it. A very bittersweet moment it must have been. There were about twenty fraternity guys who hadn't already left for summer break. We bought steaks and cigars, which were two things that Evan really enjoyed. We sat around the fire for the rest of the night. We all went around the circle of the bonfire and told personal stories about Evan and how great a person he was. Patrick came to support me and spent time with us around the bonfire, which meant a lot considering he was not even a member. Girls showed up unexpectedly throughout the evening with snacks and gifts for us, expressing their sorrow.

When it was my turn to speak around the bonfire,

I shared some stories and our last conversation with everyone. And how some of our last words were, "I love you. Have a great summer, and we will see each other next school year and continue the good times." Evan and I had become close during that year especially because we had the little bro and big bro friendship. That is what made it harder for me to take especially. We had a lifetime of memories and experiences ahead of us, and it was brutal to admit that it was no longer the case.

That day was quite possibly the hardest day of my life so far. I thought I had been through hell in high school and challenges at Key Ridge, but this was completely different. Nothing compared to losing one of my closest friends. And although that day was among the most difficult I had ever been through, it was also very special. It was special because we all came together and shared our love for Evan around the bonfire into the night until about 3:00 a.m. We shared many laughs and we shed some tears. But it was special to see how much Evan impacted each individual person in a positive way, and how much he meant to the fraternity as a whole. It was beautiful to hear each person share his or her best stories and fondest memories of Evan. And it has continued to this day and will carry on into the future. He left an unforgettable presence and legacy with us all.

The outreach and love from my family, friends, and many others on the University of Arizona campus was amazing. Not just that day and following weeks but months after. And still to this day. He positively impacted each life he came in contact with. His smile was contagious and would make you smile even on a rough day. His laugh was evident, so much so that you could hear it down the hall even when it was noisy with other conversations. His demeanor was admirable, as he cared deeply for his family, friends, and loved ones. He was always so nice and respectful to people he didn't even know. Many admired him. Evan was a special young man, one very dear to my heart. And so many other hearts in this world. His legacy will always be remembered, and he will stick with each and every one of us. He will never be forgotten because of the impact he left with people: positive, inspiring, and cheerful.

Each and every day after that, nothing was the same. Not for me. Not for any of the fraternity brothers. Not for anyone who knew Evan well. And certainly nothing would be for his family. Nothing would ever be the same. I would wake up in the morning feeling like part of me was gone. And that is how I felt each day and each night. It was very hard to progress and focus on other things in life. He was such a great person with a bright future, and it was hard for me to take it all in. It was hard for everyone. It was truly an inexplicable experience and still is and will always be. There are not enough words to do justice to the impact he had on people's lives.

My dad drove out that Monday, just two days after Evan's passing. He was coming out to help me move to Phoenix for my summer internship. My first day of work was scheduled for the following week. I was nowhere near mentally or emotionally ready to begin working a new job, especially one in sports, that I cared a lot about and was preparing myself extensively for. But it was good that my dad came out because I needed all the help I could get. He knew I was devastated. I could hardly do anything; even eating, drinking, and sleeping were challenges. My motivation and energy was low, and all I felt like doing was sleeping, even though it was hard to. When my dad got in, he helped me pack up a bit, and we got a nice dinner together. He was very supportive and understood that I was in a difficult time. The following day we did our final round of packing, and I said good-bye to everyone who was still in Tucson. We drove up to Phoenix early Friday morning.

The transition was made easier having my dad there, and the move was successful. The rest of the week we spent a lot of quality time together before he eventually flew back home five days later. I was set to start work on May 26, 2015, just ten days after Evan's passing.

I have to tell you that starting a new internship while having one of my close friends pass away just ten days prior was one of the hardest things I ever had to endure. I had to put a fake smile on. And I was nervous to start my new job too. For my entire life, I had dreamt about working for a sports team, and at the age of twenty-one, I had accomplished that. But I had to try to block everything out and just focus on the job, at least while in the office. So on Tuesday, I put on my business clothes, gathered my notebook, and went to my first day of work. When I approached the front door of the arena entrance, a few people were there to greet me. One was my manager, and the other two were going to be my fellow coworkers. Within the first five minutes, I felt more at ease and content with my decision to work there. Each person I met throughout my first day was welcoming and energetic.

After a great first week of work, I was set to fly out of Phoenix to Denver that weekend. I flew out Friday night because there was a "Celebration of Life" ceremony for Evan at his high school in Boulder on Saturday. Nearly thirty fraternity brothers traveled to Denver from all over the country to be at this service. I knew this weekend was not going to be easy. Two of the fraternity brothers were nice enough to let some of us stay at their families' houses. Their families were great to us and showed us much support.

Saturday would turn out to be one of the saddest but most memorable days of my life. When we arrived for the ceremony, hundreds of people were there to honor Evan. I would guess seven or eight hundred. It was beautiful to see the impact he had on others and the love he shared with each person there. All thirty of the fraternity brothers sat in the audience together. The entire auditorium was saddened, and every person had tissues to wipe the tears.

There were about ten speakers throughout the ceremony. As a group of his fraternity brothers, we were asked to select one or two of us to make a speech at the podium. The only reason I hesitated was because I didn't want to break down in tears in front of everyone. But I decided that I would speak, along with another brother, Haden. Before it was our turn to speak, I was bawling tears in the audience. The speeches were touching, the music was moving, and the background pictures of Evan and his life made my heart ache. My heart was racing, and I was nervous to speak, especially without having a prepared written piece. But Haden and I walked up on the stage together, looked out at the full crowd, and gave our speeches. Somehow I managed not to break down on stage. I talked about how much love I had for Evan and how close we had become, being big and little brother in the fraternity. I shared some of the greatest memories we had together. I shared the story of the time we all went camping. This happened about eight months prior, in the beginning stages of being friends with Evan. On that night, it was about 3:30 a.m., and about fifteen people were sitting around the campfire. Evan and I were two of those people. We were playing the game Questions, which is a game where the person in the center asks each person whatever they want. So when it was my turn to ask Evan a question, I asked, "What is one thing you want me to do for you as your big bro?" And he said, "Greg, just make sure we remain friends for the rest of our lives. Don't distance yourself once you graduate." I chuckled and said, "That won't be hard to do, buddy."

I explained to the audience what meaning I got from his response. Not only did it express our friendship, but also it showcased what a genuine person he was. He could have said anything at all, but he meant what he said from the bottom of his heart, and I was honored to be a part of his life and have him touch my life in such a positive way.

Haden supported me as I spoke to the audience, and I did the same for him as he spoke because it was a very difficult thing to do. We concluded our speeches, gave each other a hug, and proceeded to head back to our seats in the audience. Following our speeches, Evan's mom and dad spoke. I felt sick to my stomach because I couldn't imagine how devastating it was to lose a son. Their speeches were beautiful. When the ceremony ended, I went up to his mother. I briefly introduced myself and we wrapped each other in our arms and just cried together. We were desperately grasping each other for about twenty seconds, as it seemed too hard to let go. I will never forget that moment and how moving it was for both of us. She raised such a wonderful young man. And I told her how honored I was to have known him and be his big brother in the fraternity. The fraternity brothers took a picture with his mom in the middle and Evan's picture shown on the screen. I met his father and younger brother too, who are two amazing individuals. It was special to meet his family and be at the service for Evan.

Similar to the night around the bonfire, we all went

back to one of the friends' houses after the service and smoked cigars in honor of Evan and shared our greatest memories of him. As hard as that weekend was, it was so meaningful to me, and I was thankful that I was able to be at the service and present a speech. It was something that will always have a place in my heart.

I flew back to Phoenix on Sunday. Looking back on the weekend, it was a special and much-needed experience. Although still deeply saddened, I felt good to have met his family and spent time with them. I was grateful that everyone thought of Evan as such a charismatic and wonderful human being.

The next day was Monday, and it was my first full week of the internship. There were seven interns that summer, all of whom I worked very closely with. We all received extensive training before we hit the phones to call our clients. That entire summer I learned so much about sales and how to fulfill a job to its utmost capability. I worked hard and tried to absorb every piece of information that someone would tell me. It turned out that I loved my job and loved the people I was working with. The work environment was great, and it was interesting to face challenges in order to obtain success. I became close with the employees. One person served as the mentor to the seven interns. We would work with this person one-on-one for self-development on sales. He suggested I read a book called *Marketing Outrageously* by Jon Spoelstra. At the time, I wasn't a big reader, but I took his advice and read the book. Not knowing what to expect, I was blown away. In fact, I was so blown away by the book that I decided to e-mail Mr. Spoelstra asking what he did at a young age to set him up for his future success. A little background information: Jon Spoelstra is considered by many to be one of the top marketers in the world. I sent the e-mail with a mind-set of, What do I have to lose? I knew there was a very likely chance he would never even read it, let alone respond to me directly. But two hours later, I received an e-mail. I open it, and I could not believe my eyes. It was from Jon Spoelstra himself. He even addressed the e-mail using my name. I was shocked but so excited. He answered my question about what he did early on to set him up for success.

I printed out the e-mail conversation between Jon and I, and I brought it into work the next day. I showed it to our mentor. He was beside himself and very proud of me for doing that.

Although it was difficult balancing the emotions following the passing of Evan, the entire internship would end up going very well. I learned a great deal and had a tremendous experience along the way. Following the internship, it was time to go back to school.

I have continued to do well in the business school while enjoying the college lifestyle. Everything with the fraternity has been going great but is definitely not the same without our dear friend Evan. I have become very close with his family. They came to Tucson to visit for family weekend. It was great for them to see what Evan was a part of during his year at the school and in the fraternity because they knew he loved it so much. During that weekend, we did something especially memorable. We all gathered together on a beautiful Sunday morning and buried part of Evan's ashes in a serene part of the yard. It has a beautiful stone on top of it with his name, and the words "Beloved Brother and Friend." His family was all for this, and they wanted his legacy to keep living on in the fraternity, so we did just that. His family was forever grateful, and we are forever grateful for them and to have known Evan. I finished that remaining semester strong and entered 2016 excited and eager to see what was to come. But never did I know just how special one year could be.

23

Bon Voyage

In January 2016, my friends and I began planning our spring break trip for March. We were considering many ideas: Lake Havasu, Mexico, Southern California, Las Vegas, etc. But then came an idea from my friend to go on a five-day cruise to Catalina and Ensenada, Mexico. It sounded intriguing, so we looked into it, and we eventually bought tickets because it was too good of a deal to pass up. So once my last midterm ended in March, I flew from Tucson to LAX and would spend the first weekend with my folks before heading on the cruise for the next five days. What I didn't realize is how extraordinary and eye opening this week would be for me going forward.

The flight from Tucson to LAX is only an hour and fifteen minutes long. My friend dropped me off at the airport, and I went through security, awaiting to board Southwest. When it was boarding time, I picked a seat in the middle of the plane. I was the only one in my row at that point. Usually when I go on flights, I wait to see who sits next to me to see if I can strike up a conversation with them first. And if they don't seem into it, then I just put my headphones in and listen to music. So there I was, patiently waiting to see which stranger would take the empty seat next to me in the middle, since I had the ever-so-glamorous window seat. After about ten minutes, a tall man with glasses, brown hair and a Green Bay Packers hat sat next to me.

"Hi, sir, how about those Packers?" I said. He chuckled and introduced himself. "I see you go the University of Arizona," he said. He was referring to the polo shirt I was wearing with our school logo on it. We got to talking. He asked me about my studies, where I was from, and what I wanted to do later on with my career. I asked him what he did and if he had kids who went the U of A. He said no, but he said he had a son and a daughter, one of whom went to a small Christian school in Ohio and the other a small Christian school in California. And when he said small, he meant small. I assumed a few thousand people, and he explained that each school only had a few hundred students. Five minutes later, he checked the time on his iPhone. Out of the corner of my eye, I saw his screensaver was a picture of Jesus Christ.

Since we were already on the topic of his two kids going to Christian schools, I began to converse more in depth with the man. I politely asked about his screensaver. I could tell by his demeanor that he was not shy and was open to talk about his faith in God since I was curious. I admitted to him that I was essentially clueless about what any of that meant. I told him I believed in God or a higher power, but that was about it. Never practiced, never really prayed, was never baptized, and hadn't read one line of the Bible. I was a big-time sinner in many respects. But in general, I tend to be a curious, open-minded person on any matter, even sensitive subjects. So I asked away. And he was excited to talk to me and answer my questions. I was nervous and at times uncomfortable since I couldn't relate to him at all.

But I will never ever forget that hour-and-fifteen-minute conversation with this man. I learned so much about faith, Jesus, and what it means to be a devoted Christian just in that short time. I didn't even really know the difference between a Christian, Catholic, Jew, etc., at the time. All my spiritual life consisted of at the time was opening presents on Christmas and eating Peeps on Easter. I was that much of a rookie. But he explained to me how it's more than praying or reading the Bible. It's how he has a relationship with the Lord. It's how he keeps the Lord at the center focus of his life at all times. It's that he has surrendered his life to him and admits the Lord is his savior and is always forgiving of one's sins. The man admitted that he is not perfect and that he messes up. That goes for every human. And it is okay to mess up because nobody on this planet is perfect. But he explained the fine line between thinking you are good enough and that you earn greatness from God, versus admitting you are not worthy enough, only for God to love you more. All of this was new to me. My head was spinning. I felt overwhelmed and confused. I couldn't relate to this man at all. My only goal for this conversation was to be a sponge and absorb all the information that I could. And who knew? Maybe this guy was full of crap and I didn't realize it. But I just took the chance, listened to what he had to say, and absorbed his explanations.

At the end of the flight, we both told each other that we were very touched by one another. He touched me by being so open with me, especially because we were strangers. And he was touched by me as I was open-minded and asked questions about something he deeply cares about. The best thing of all was that I felt he actually cared for me, even as a stranger. He cared to share his faith with someone who was not faithfully strong. He wanted to positively impact my life by sharing how good the Lord is. When we said our good-byes, he offered to give me his e-mail address and phone number.

I declined. Even though we had just shared a great, long talk, my thought was still that this guy was a stranger, and in reality I didn't really know who he was as a person, other than what we talked about. So I declined.

I walked off the plane with my head thinking a thousand thoughts. I was very moved by this man and our conversation. But I was also very intimidated and nervous. I felt inferior and bad about myself. I kind of just brushed it off, kept it to myself, and approached my parents waiting at the airport as if nothing happened.

"Bon Voyage!" Two days later, I left on the cruise with five of my good buddies from the U of A. We were so excited to get away for a while and have some fun. There were a lot of college students on the cruise, especially from the U of A. The first day was a blast. We got some great drinks, went in the pool, won an auction at an art show on board, gambled, ate lots of delicious food, saw a comedy show, and went to the night club. It wasn't just the first day that was a blast, but every day and every night.

On the evening of the first night, one of my friends (who is one of the most outgoing people I know) kind of roamed off by himself and met these two girls. I later met them that night in the nightclub. One of them really caught my attention. She was petite with long legs. Her hair was brown with golden tips and had a luscious, wavy style to it. Her face was cute beyond belief. She had brown, marble eyes to go with a charming smile. She was dressed in classy, luxurious looking clothes. And her charisma made me want to get to know her. This girl had a glow to her that was unlike anything else. She told me she went by

V. The only problem was that my friend got to talk to her well before I did, so I just took a backseat and enjoyed the time with the rest of the guys. We all ended up having a great time that night.

The following evening we ate a formal dinner in the main dining room. Little did I know, my friend invited V and her other girlfriend to eat dinner with us. We sat across the large, circular table from one another. I was just trying to enjoy the moment with everyone and not go out of my way to talk to her, especially because my friend was sitting next to her. I didn't want to seem pushy.

But later that night, things began to change. After a long, fun night of dancing with all our friends, V and I found ourselves on the back balcony of the ship together. Everyone else either headed to bed or went to go gamble, so V and I ordered a pizza from the bistro and took it out to the balcony, where the crisp, ocean breeze filled our faces. The sound of the ship sailing along the waves was peaceful as we gazed miles out into the darkness, where we couldn't see a single thing. Just she and I.

All I knew was that I had a warm, delicious pizza on the table and the most elegant and charming girl right next to me. I couldn't mess this one up.

As we began conversation, I didn't feel nervous at all. I barely knew this girl, but there was something about her that made me comfortable and at ease. She was so kind-hearted and caring. It was easy to tell even from just a few minutes of talking.

Five hours later, I still found myself on the back balcony of the ship talking with V. Not bored, not eager to leave, just a bit tired. It was 5:15 a.m., and we had not moved. We were at that table on the balcony for the entire night. We were in each other's presence and enjoying the special moment. I learned a lot about V, including that it was her twenty-fifth birthday that very night.

We had almost every conversation you could think of within that five-hour time span. From her birthday, to our educations, to our career paths, to even our life stories and struggles, it was all so fulfilling. And then I found out ... V was a devoted Christian and follower of the Lord.

When I heard that, many thoughts came rushing to my head. The first one was, "Oh, this girl is too mature and out of my league. She'll never give the time of day to a guy who isn't a Christian." But the most prominent of all was the reminiscence of the man on the plane, just a few days earlier. I began to think to myself: I never had one single Christian friend in my life, and now all of a sudden, two Christian people enter my life in very unique circumstances.

I told V the story about my experience with the man on the plane. She was so moved, and her smile lit up her beautiful face. She told me that she thought this was happening for a reason, that these things don't just happen without a purpose, that God was trying to teach me something. My head began to race. I actually agreed with her. I knew in my heart that this wasn't happening just to happen. There had to be something behind all of this, right?

About two hours out of the five consisted of V and I talking about the Lord, her faith, the man on the plane, and Christianity. Again, I was basically a rookie, besides my encounter four days prior. But I loved how she was so forgiving and open minded, even to a guy like me who was a nonfollower of Christ. She treated me so well and didn't look down upon me. For some reason, I had a false preconception that all religious people alienated nonfollowers of the Lord. But she didn't. She was encouraging and helpful. I learned a lot from her that night, not just about her as a person but a lot about where her heart and mind were. And even though all this was new and surprising to me, I had a burning desire to get to know V and spend time with her. And I had a burning desire to also ask her questions about her relationship with the Lord. The subject easily could have intimidated me, but I saw something greater here. I just knew there was more to this than just a conversation on a plane and a conversation on a cruise ship.

Around 5:15 a.m., we wrapped up our conversation, and I gave her a birthday hug and said goodnight. We went to our separate rooms, only to wake up two and a half hours later to get off at the port of Catalina Island. Some nap that was.

The whole group had a great time exploring Catalina. V and I met up again and told one another how moved we were by what happened the night before. She ended up having a great birthday, and we celebrated with a couple of splendid mimosas on the island.

The remaining couple of days on the cruise were fantastic as well. Besides getting seasick a few times, the trip was one of the most fun experiences I've had. V and I continued talking and spending time together the last couple of days on the cruise, in a very casual manner. I was very curious to see what would happen after this trip. I knew in my head that I wanted to stay in contact, even if that meant just being friends. In my head, I saw something potentially more than friends, but I had no idea what she thought. My first guess was that she probably thought it'd be cool to stay friends but nothing more serious than that, especially because I wasn't a Christian. I was even afraid that we would lose contact all together.

Saying good-bye to V on the final night of the cruise was beyond difficult. I knew I had to see this girl again at some point. But I was afraid it would be my last conversation with her — our last words, our last hug, and our last good-bye.

Once I returned to Tucson three days later, I decided to text her. What did I have to lose? The initial conversations went well, and it was so nice to be in touch again. We began texting much more often and things seemed to be going well. Then we started to Facetime each other every now and then, which was great. I started to really know in my heart there was some mutual interest. Sometimes we would have three- or four-hour-long conversations, which we loved every minute of. V and I began to grow close, even though I was in Tucson and she was still back at her home in California.

But not only was progress made with V but with something else just as important. Following the cruise, I began to think to myself that there had to be a reason I met the guy on the plane and V in a matter of four days. And how each of them touched my life in such special ways but more because they were both Christians and followers of the Lord. I just knew in my heart that something was happening. I viewed these as signals that I would be foolish to overlook. So I decided to take action. Again, what did I have to lose? I was just curious as to why the cards were aligning as they were. So I decided to contact one of my old friends from the dorm my freshman year of college. I always knew he was a devoted Christian. I reached out to him and asked him to go to lunch so we could catch up.

A few days later, we met up and talked for a few hours. He was surprised to hear that I was reaching out in regards to learning more about the Lord. But he was filled with joy.

During the remaining semester of spring 2016, he helped me grow immensely. I told him that I wanted to learn more about God and develop my faith. We would sit down each week and talk about the Lord and how we as people can change our lives if we keep God as our center-piece. We would read the Bible, which felt like a foreign language to me and was somewhat overwhelming at first. At this point, I viewed our meetings as a time to analyze if I wanted to live for God or not, since I was so new to all of this. I didn't think I would. I thought it would be too chal-lenging, too difficult to refrain from sin and too boring of a lifestyle. I was afraid to lose friends, and even family. I was afraid of the life change.

Slowly but surely over time, I started to become more committed in my faith. I realized that it was all worth it. And the cool thing was that I still have kept my friends, which I was terrified wouldn't happen. I am still friends with straights, gays, blacks, whites, Asians, Hispanics, Jews, Catholics, atheists, Muslims, Christians, etc. I don't judge anyone differently because different people have different priorities, which is their own personal decision.

In developing my faith, I have grown from saying I wanted to change to actually acting on it. I began to change my mind, my actions, and my heart to be centered on the Lord. From praying to reading the Bible and other Christian books to diminishing sin as best as I could. I was surprised when I realized that I knew in my heart that I wanted to live for God. I never envisioned this. I thought being a good person was good enough in life. I am now a Christian and follower of the Lord, but that doesn't make me perfect or better than anyone else. I am still just as flawed as all of us in this world. But I have accepted, and have surrendered that to the Lord.

With the influence of the man on the plane, V, and now

meeting with my friend, I began to grow a lot in my faith in a matter of a few months. I became a Christian. And, man, let me tell you, it has not been easy. From resisting temptation, lust, and making countless other sacrifices, the entire growing experience has really opened my eyes. Some realizations have been painful and difficult to understand, like how it should be natural for one to love God more than your significant other. It was hard to grasp for a while, but now I understand why. Nothing matters and nothing exists without God. Many other things have been hard to understand too, but God is our savior, as he died on the cross for us all. That's what matters. He wants us to love him, follow him, and admit our sins and wrongdoings so we can be forgiven. He wants us to surrender our lives and put them in the hands of his own. He wants us to admit we're not perfect instead of trying to earn our way to heaven by being a good person. As we live in this difficult and tempting world, he will bless us with grace as long as we love him, follow him, and honor him in all that we do.

I never ever imagined this, for me to commit to living for the Lord. But I am forever thankful for V, the man on the plane, and my friend for helping me learn. But the most credit of all goes to the Lord himself, who put those people in my life for a reason, to open my mind to something I was oblivious to. God touched my life by using those three people as influences. And oh, how it has been the most incredible experience coming to the Lord. It has indeed changed my life for the better. V and I have a great and healthy relationship with each other, centered on the Lord. She has continued to help me grow in my faith and Christianity.

Now, looking back, I really wish I accepted the offer

from the man on the plane to have his contact information. I never thought I would be in this position, and yet it all started from him. I wish I could reach out to him and say thank you. I wish I could tell him about my journey of coming to the Lord. I am forever thankful for where my life has gone, from my dark high school days to living a life with God.

Now I must mention that my goal isn't to persuade you to come to God. That is not my place. That is your decision. There will be opportunities for you whenever they present themselves. My purpose for writing about my coming of faith is to show you how powerful and life changing it can be. What I want you to get out of this is to make sure to always keep an open mind. You never know when something in life is going to happen to you for a reason, for a real purpose. If I were close-minded, I would have shut off the man on the plane and V and would have not reached out to my friend back at college. Not only would I not be close to God, but I wouldn't even have my wonderful girlfriend in my life. I would not be where I am now. So with anything in life, don't jump to conclusions and assume something isn't for you just because you are inexperienced and unknowledgeable on the subject matter. Consider your options, keep an open mind, and learn about whatever it is. Then, once you truly understand the given circumstances, you can make a decision on whether or not you want to keep pursuing it.

A similar analogy is applying for jobs. If someone only is set on one company or one job, he or she won't understand what else is out there. One very well could like something even better than what he or she is currently doing. I realized that living for God is infinitely more fulfilling than anything else I was doing prior. So if that person had an open mind and was willing to learn and to decide if the change is right, then opportunities and fulfillment can become endless. That goes for anything in life.

Recently, there have been some exciting things going on. I joined a Christian group on campus and have met some unbelievable people there. A couple people in particular are becoming very dear friends of mine. I committed to a church. V and I continue to have a terrific relationship. I love that girl more than I can put into words. Not just for her beauty, charm, love, care, inspiration, joy, humor, and positivity, but for touching my heart and bringing me to the Lord.

I completed my first "corporate-world" internship, which was an unbelievable experience. This marks my final internship as I finish up my last academic year and prepare for my postcollegiate career.

Josh recently finished up his senior year at McKinney High School. He did very well in school and had an abundance of close friends. I am so relieved that he had an enjoyable experience at McKinney High because I was nervous for him after what I went through. But everyone is different, and he made the most of his time there.

We received wonderful news that Josh got accepted to the University of Arizona. He proudly committed to be a Wildcat and just recently started his freshman year! This was always one of my dreams to have him at the school during my final year of college. Not only did he come to U of A, but he joined my fraternity as well! It has been a great time so far, and we look forward to more good times to come. Another major change is that I picked up a double major in entrepreneurship. The McGuire Center for Entrepreneurship is a top-five-ranked program nationally. It is just the beginning, but it has been a blast so far, and I look forward to what happens as the year carries on. My mom and dad are doing very well. My dad has been eligible to retire for a few months now but has continued to work. My mom remains occupied with family and has been enjoying herself.

This year, along with every other year, has been special in its own way. But let me tell you, the last two years have been busy, balancing school, social life, the McGuire Entrepreneurship Program, having internships, writing this book, having V in my life, and committing to the Lord. But I truly feel blessed by each one of these and many others because just a few years ago, nobody, including my family and myself, thought I would be in the position of having these opportunities. I have learned throughout my college experience to make the most of every opportunity, to have a balanced lifestyle of work and fun, and most of all, to enjoy life.

24

Reflection

I think about life all the time, the past, present, and future. And every time I look back on the past and reflect, it never fails to amaze me. The ups and downs and the good and bad are all equally special and important. I know I have had some damn rough times. But do you know what? I wouldn't change it for anything. Because I would not be the same person I am today without enduring the challenges that I faced in life. Everyone has a special story. Everyone is special in his or her own way. And there is a reason why I chose to spend over two years writing this book. I want you to learn from my story and improve your life. Not a lot of people manage to screw up their own lives, and I nearly did. Yeah, I was depressed. Yeah, I had no self-confidence. Yeah, I got obsessed over a girl. Yeah, dealing with my coach was a hard time. But the bottom line is that no matter what those external factors were or how depressed I was, I had control over my decisions. I had control of whether or not to step out on that ledge. And believe me, I was at rock bottom and utterly depressed. And it was so, so hard to push through and try to find the good in life. While battling depression, all I wanted to do was go to sleep and never wake up.

But still, at the end of the day, I had control over my body and my decision-making. And instead of seeking help or trying to meet new friends, I just would put my head down and sulk and unleash tears in the high school bathroom. Although it is very hard to control depression, the bottom line is that I was still in control if I believed that I was in control. But I didn't believe, and I let it get the best of me, and it took me over. I was no longer Greg Vogt. I was no longer my positive, happy self. I was a completely different person than I am now. I was shut down, and I wanted life to end because I saw that there was no meaning for me in this world anymore. No meaning for myself and no meaning for others to have me. I did not feel wanted here. And that is why I attempted suicide. It's because I had no self-control or self-worth. If I just had tried to have self-worth, just made an attempt to love myself, then I would have made another decision instead of resorting to attempting suicide. But instead, I would allow my depression to pile up and get out of control. I was trapped in a bubble that I could not escape. I had no vision beyond it. And I didn't ask for help. I repeat: I didn't ask for help. My parents put me in therapy, but I didn't want to be there. It was my attitude … a terrible one. It wasn't their fault or anyone else's. It was my fault. I never took control of my decisions. If I just had an open mind, who knows what could have changed? But I let this depression completely control my life. It was a demon, and I will never, ever forget that feeling. And as a result of not controlling my depression, I could have died. I very well could not be here right now. And I am beyond thankful that I made it through those dark days.

I am beyond thankful for my family and the friends who helped me along the way. I am thankful for Key Ridge, because as hard as it was, it changed my life infinitely for the better. And now, I am beyond thankful for the University of Arizona, my fraternity, V, and all the wonderful friends I have met along the way. I am most thankful for God. I have grown a lot, and I would not be here without that support system. But even still, I cost my family and friends heartache, pain, and suffering. I made my little brother be without his role model for a year. I made my parents be without their son for a year. And now I realize what I did. I realize that I was selfish. If I was able to cure it with changing my habits to ultimately change my life, then you sure as hell can accomplish whatever you put your mind to. I have lived through it, and that is what I believe. If you take control, you will accomplish whatever that is.

Now, here is my main point, depression aside. If you are to get one thing out of reading this book, here it is: Life will bring you struggles. Life will bring you good times. But during the challenges, it is all about perception and making the rational decision. The bottom line is that you are in control of your life, and if it is not going the way you want it to, it is up to you to make the necessary changes in your life to improve it on where you envision it to be. You must take control and not be your own worst enemy.

I have battled through three painful years of depression, not knowing how to change my life. I have experienced fourteen deaths in my twenty-three years of living. And those fourteen people were people I was close to. Grandparents, friends, teachers, neighbors, friends at Key Ridge, and more. A couple due to suicide, others old age, some drugs, some freak accidents. Nobody should ever experience that much heartache. And it has taken its toll on me. Death is one of the most painful things to endure, and it is hard each and every time, especially when you are really close to the person. The combination of my severe depression in high school and the tragedies

I have endured was a daunting, improbable obstacle to overcome. But I eventually grew the courage to seek help at Key Ridge and meet new friends. I put myself out there to make the change. I took control before it was too late. Slowly I gained confidence and things got better one by one. Miraculously, I was able to permanently be off the medications and will no longer ever be on them. I am now living a fulfilling life and enjoying my college experience. Much credit goes to the people who have helped me along the way. But I might not be here right now if I had never learned that I needed to make my own decisions to better my own life. The biggest thing I have ever done in my life was admitting that I was not happy and taking action to change my own life for the better.

It is now January 2017. I am writing to you from the library at the University of Arizona. To this day, I have not seen or heard from either Coach Norris or Sofia. I have not reached out to either of them myself. The last time I saw Coach Norris was when I poured water on him after the final game of the season and the two of us proceeded to get into a major altercation. The last time I saw Sofia was when I walked out of class, threw my legs over the railing of the third-story building, and contemplated jumping. I have had people ask me, "What would you say if you ever ran into Sofia again?" For years, this was a different answer. If this was when I was fifteen or sixteen, I would have said something like, "I wished you liked me." Or, "You were part of the reason all this happened." But now I have a whole new perspective. I would apologize to her because I do feel like I acted selfishly toward her. She did nothing wrong. Absolutely nothing. She already had a boyfriend and was still a very nice, supportive friend to me. I just didn't see the good in that. I took it for granted because I wanted more. So I would apologize to her and explain how she didn't deserve what I put her through.

It has been over five years since I have been off the anti-depressant medications. I have not been depressed in over five years, and I am a happy, content individual. I have accomplished a lot in my life since making the decision to go off the medications. And although life still throws its challenges at me all the time, I have resiliency and know how to handle situations. My past experiences have taught me what it's like to face major obstacles, but I now know how to turn those situations into a positive when the opportunity presents itself. I have become mentally strong from what I went through.

Even after McKinney High School and Key Ridge, I have dealt with very difficult situations, particularly the passing of Evan. It has made me learn to try to model my life to keep a positive perspective each and every day. I feel blessed that I was a friend with such a great person, Evan. I feel blessed with how my life has turned out. I am thankful for all my family and friends, and I am thankful for each day I wake up.

And now I will leave you with one final thought before my thirteen tips. I can make all the excuses that I want about my past. About how I was depressed, verbally bullied, had a bad relationship with my coach, and got obsessed over a girl. All those things happened, and they were rough. But instead of making excuses, I decided to take the negatives and turn them into positives. I wanted my life to change for the better, so I made decisions in order to do that. And if I can turn my life from being at rock bottom to now living a wonderful life, you and anyone else on this planet can too. You are in control of your life and the decisions you make, no matter what they may be.

In order for you to live a fulfilling life, you must find the good in both life's challenges and positive times. Ride out the good times for as long as you can. But during the hard times, make sure you create a vision on how to overcome the challenges and take control. If you don't take control, you'll be facing the battle against yourself.

25

My Thirteen Tips for You

Although I am only twenty-three years old, I feel that I have gained valuable experiences and lessons in life through enduring my hardships and facing learning situations. These thirteen tips are applicable to any person's life, no matter the age, demographic, or personal background. My hope is that you consider my words and apply these lessons to take control and improve your life.

Here are my thirteen tips to living a life full of happiness, success, and fulfillment:

1.   **Learn to love yourself.** Before you do anything else or try to accomplish whatever goals you have, you must first love yourself. If one does not love him or herself, then nothing else matters. It is your life, and you must appreciate who you are in order to capitalize on everything life has to offer. Self-confidence will take you a long way. Learn to love yourself by becoming the best version of yourself instead of comparing yourself to others.

2.   **Be kind to others.** Though it is essential to have self-worth, showing genuine care toward other people will dramatically improve your life. I was selfish as a teenager, but I have learned to look out for other people's best interests, especially the people

that matter the most. Being kind is something so simple, yet in today's society, I feel like people often struggle with this. Making somebody else feel good about him or herself is a special thing.

3. **Master the seesaw effect.** Picture a seesaw in the middle of a park. One side of it goes up while the other goes down. Some of this movement is caused by external factors such as heavy winds or if a big ball hits one side down or if a random person comes and uses their own force to push it one way. It also consists of internal factors. I classify the internal factors as the objects directly and intentionally interfering with the seesaw. That object is you. Except you have the ability to control both sides. Because the seesaw is your life. And you control all sides and ends of the spectrum. There is not another person on the other side. To make the seesaw even, you must have balance. If you're sitting on one side, you must find a way to make the other side even out. You must do the right things and have strategies to balance the seesaw when you are in control of it. This is how life works. We tend to have so much on our plates and so many stressors in our lives that we forget how to balance stress, family, friends, fun, work, and priorities. But balance is one of the most important aspects to having a happy and fulfilling life. If I had a balanced mind-set in high school, you wouldn't even be reading this sentence right now because this book wouldn't have been a thing. I would have been better rounded and would have had different priorities than basketball and Sofia. But I was too one-dimensional and closed off. And

due to a lack of balance, I spiraled out of control. Literally. I guess it ironically helped me in the long run since I was able to write this book, but you get my point. Things got terrible, nearly life ending. But balance would have changed everything. I would have been less worked up about two things and more focused and well rounded on a variety. But no, I said "screw you" to balance. Don't do what I did. Have balance. Be mindful of your thinking, your priorities, and your actions. And make it happen. Be the one who controls the seesaw. This is just an analogy I came up with, but I believe it is relevant and important to master. Don't let the seesaw or any external factors control you.

4. **For every bad thing that happens, there are at least three positive things.** This is important to remember, especially during tough times. When people are upset, they often spiral into an irrational state of mind and think that only bad things are happening to them. But in reality, life is great and precious, and we need to remember to appreciate the little things in life. Do not take anything for granted. When you are upset, make sure to think about the great things in your life that you are truly appreciative of, whether that is good health, friendships, family, fun experiences, or anything else that makes you happy.

5. **Be ambitious, and try new things.** This is a great way to learn to take control of your life. Get out of your comfort zone. Take some risks within reason. Be ambitious. Try new things. You never know what good things can come along later on by experimen-

tation. Keep an open mind. You won't know your potential if you don't try.

6. **Go with your gut.** I contemplated writing this book for six months before actually writing my first word. I was afraid of people's judgments, as well as the daunting time commitment. But I had a strong gut feeling that writing this book was the right thing to do, so I did it. And it took me over two years, but I knew I should go with my gut to get it done. Don't let people dissuade you from what you believe is right.

7. **Think big, but take baby steps.** You won't accomplish your big goals overnight. Making small gains toward your goal is essential to success. For years, my goal was to overcome my depression. But it took me three full years, which was a long time. I tried new things in order to make small improvements to reach my larger goal. It paid off, as I haven't had depression in over five years. Now I have other big goals, such as writing this book, getting a great career and following God. I am working by taking baby steps each day to reach the larger goal. Have a vision of your big goal always in mind, but target that big goal each day by making small strides. Nothing worth it in life comes easy, right?

8. **Think on the positive side.** There is no point of always complaining about the negatives going on in your life, because that will only make things worse. Having a positive mind-set and attitude is key to personal happiness. It will rub off in a good way on everyone around you. Attract what you want

by being what you want. This is done by staying positive (unless you want negativity around you).

9. **Never settle.** You will not be happy and fully content if you settle, whether that is with relationships, jobs, experiences, or setting goals. It is important to know your worth and strive for what you desire. If you don't settle, you won't complain. If you don't settle, you will be thankful. Being thankful and not complaining are important parts of life. A great way to practice making sure you aren't settling is by learning from your past mistakes.

10. **Don't judge a book by its cover.** People often jump to conclusions about a person when they really know very little about them. Part of the reason I sought to write this book was to try to create a lesson to form a societal change. And that is to really get to know someone before making any assumptions about them. Just because you see a beautiful person with expensive clothes on doesn't mean they're cocky and spoiled. Get to know them. Or just because someone you know is usually happy and well doesn't mean he or she isn't suffering through a personal battle. Get to know them. Everybody is up against some sort of battle, so it is very important to be sympathetic and not to preconceive people.

11. **Identify your life's purpose, and capitalize on what sets you apart from the rest.** Think about it. Write down your goals and priorities. Strategize. Make it happen. Don't sit down and watch life pass you by, because it will. I had three miserable years of my life that I could have made happy and memo-

rable. But I chose to not be in control. I wasn't myself in high school. I was somebody else. I did nothing to set myself apart. It eventually ate me away and threw me into a scary depression. Whether it's being happy, healthy, successful, loving, caring, ambitious, or whatever you choose, you must do things that set you apart and make you your own person. Identify what is unique about you and use it to your advantage. Just like a job interview. You try your best to set yourself apart from the competition. Have that mind-set in other aspects of life. Because if you don't, you will be limiting your opportunities for personal growth.

12. **Do what makes you happy.** Happiness is one of the most important aspects to get out of this thing we call life. So do what makes you happy, even if that means making sacrifices. And if you need help with something, then ask for help, because happy is how life should be lived. You will be thankful for your own personal happiness, and other people will be glad to see you happy.

13. **Admit what you are doing wrong.** This is the last point for a reason. Once you close this book, I want this to be the final thought you are left with. This is often a difficult thing to do, but admitting when you are wrong or that you are the problem can be a revolutionary change for you. It forces you to realize what you have done and take ownership and control of your decisions. It prevents the battle against yourself.

Acknowledgments

Special thanks to Wheatmark, Inc. for making this book possible. I want to thank my family, most importantly my mom, dad, and little brother for always being there and showing unconditional love. Thank you to my fraternity brothers, who have helped with my personal growth and an unforgettable college experience. Thank you to my freshman-year roommate and close friends among the University of Arizona community. Thank you to Evan and his family. Thank you to my test readers. Thank you to my friends, mentors, coaches, and professors. Thank you to staff members and peers for being there for me when I was away from home for a year. Thank you to the people I have lost throughout my life. You are all dearly missed. Thank you to the people who created hardship and adversity because I would not be who I am without going through that. Most recent, thank you V for your continuous blessings and love. And last but not least, I want to thank God for his everlasting grace and always guiding me along the way. Thank you all.

CPSIA information can be obtained
at www.ICGtesting.com
Printed in the USA
FFOW02n1200050317
33039FF